YOUR STORY
FOR
HIS GLORY

CARRIE H. PASCH

ISBN 978-1-64515-571-3 (hardcover)
ISBN 978-1-64515-572-0 (digital)

Christian Faith Publishing, Inc.
832 Park Avenue
Meadville, PA 16335
www.christianfaithpublishing.com

Cover Design: Chyntia Puspitasari
Cover Photography: Danny Sanchez Photography
Cover Make-up & Hair Styling: Lambs & Wolves, Red Bank, NJ

Printed in the United States of America

To my beloved husband, Brian Pasch.

CONTENTS

FOREWORD

Your Story For His Glory is an authentically penned, personal look into Carrie's very real walk with the Lord. I've had the privilege of knowing the woman behind the writer and calling her a friend. Not only is she now an accomplished author, but she truly lives the life you read about within these pages.

Carrie has a heart to build the kingdom and a love for others that has impacted so many people. I have witnessed the recipients of her faith expressed in love, and I know that it has left many feeling overwhelmed with gratitude. Hers is a love without judgement that is compelled by Christ's love for us.

Throughout this collection of reflections on life and learning is evidence of Carrie's knowledge applied, which is outworked as wisdom. From Bible verses to worship lyrics to snapshots into her past with epilepsy, Carrie uses them all in her writing to demonstrate her heart for God and for His people.

There is victory in vulnerability, so I love that Carrie is transparent and real. It provides the reader with incredible inspiration and insight. She doesn't shrink back from sharing all the ways she has grown and changed for the better over the course of her lifetime. Her writing is relatable and truthful: a picture of a life that has been transformed by the power of an everlasting Savior.

I left this story of her life encouraged and challenged to grow in my own relationship with God. I know that you will too.

—Keira Smallcombe, Lead Pastor of VIVE Church

INTRODUCTION

This book started as a personal journal with no intent of ever becoming a public document.

Once my husband planted the seed in my heart that he thought my writings were more than just journal entries, and that I should highly consider sharing and publishing them, I began to pray on that idea.

Publishing a book would definitely be something outside my comfort zone, but the more and more I prayed, it became clear that it's not about me. I am here *because* of God, and I am here *for* God.

I will do anything to help spread His Word and love to others, and in any way He calls me to do it—even if it's outside my comfort zone.

Did I ever think that I would write a book? Never! But here we are, my personal reflections, experiences, and spiritual growth written in these pages.

I pray that you enjoy reading my story, and that it encourages you to write *Your Story for His Glory!*

AWAKENING

You found me in the darkness
Wanderin' thru the desert
I was a hopeless fool
Now I'm hopelessly devoted
My chains are broken
And it all began with You
When love broke thru

—TobyMac

My hearts first awakening to God's true presence was about nine years ago. I always believed in God, was baptized in the Catholic church, and attended Sunday school growing up, but soon after the time of my confirmation, I stopped going to church, except for holidays. I didn't really feel a connection with God. Everything up until that time had felt very rule-and-process oriented. As a result, I started drifting away from God.

Fast-forward twenty-plus years to 2009, a very difficult year for me in several ways. I was involved in an unhealthy relationship. I was undergoing a lot of stress with my job at the time. Most importantly, I was experiencing major health issues.

I have been epileptic my whole life and take medicine daily for my condition. However, when asked by others about my seizure history, I always find it hard to explain. I can't remember because I was so young at the time of my last seizure, around five years old. It's clear I have some kind of condition, but I can't really explain anything about it. It's strange.

Well, that all changed in 2009, when my neurologist and I decided that maybe it was time to try a new medicine. This new medicine is known to have the same effectiveness as my current medicine, plus potentially lower side effects should I want to try to have children. In addition to this, it would be a good opportunity to see if I had outgrown my seizures completely.

About three months into the new medicine, I had a breakthrough seizure at the gym. Training for a half marathon on the treadmill, I suddenly blacked out and flew backwards off the machine! People who were nearby rushed over to help. I had hit my head and had a small bump on it for a few days, but that was it. No broken bones, concussion, or other physical trauma. I remembered thinking that even though I was humiliated, I was so grateful to be okay and not seriously injured.

Minutes after, the fear set in. I became so scared of this happening again—never knowing when—that fear started to overtake my body with every step I took. Would another seizure happen? It could come at any moment. Fear controlled me. How can I go out in a public place again? How can I drive? So I didn't. For several weeks, I couldn't get behind the wheel. Thankfully, my wonderful parents drove me everywhere I needed to go, including to work every single day.

My doctor and I decided to stay on the new medicine but increase the dose a bit. I was doing well on the new regimen and started to gain my confidence back a little more each day. At the same time, it seemed like getting back to my old self was taking forever, until one event in particular expedited my confidence to move forward and not live in fear—the half marathon I had been training for.

It was the night before the race, and I hadn't run distance in a while. I remember telling my father how conflicted I felt inside. I explained how I was scared I wouldn't make it through the entire race without having a seizure, but I didn't want to let all the people down who had sponsored me to run for a charity. I had committed to the race for them, and they supported me through their donations. I felt terrible.

My father said that he was sure everyone would understand my situation if I decided not to run, as long as I explained why. That didn't sit well with me, and my father could tell. So he said that he would run the race with me. He would be by my side should any-thing happen. My father hadn't run more than five miles in over ten years, but he ran with me on race day. Every step of the 13.1 miles. In the pouring rain.

Not only was I so grateful for my sweet father, but my per-sistence to move forward in life, even if it was something small like a race, started making me say to myself, "I won't let this condition stop me from being me."

Running and finishing that particular race was rewarding for me physically, but more so emotionally. I started to feel like myself again and was able to put the past in the past, so agreeing to go hit some tennis balls with my uncle, didn't require a second thought!

It was now summer in New Jersey, and my uncle and I were hit-ting back-and-forth on the clay courts, when suddenly, I blinked my eyes and realized two men were carrying me, literally lifting me up by each arm and sitting me on a white picnic chair. What happened? It didn't take more than a few seconds for me to come to my senses. I knew the answer. I'd had another seizure.

I started to cry and apologize to my uncle and the other amaz-ing gentleman that was helping him carry me. Once again, I was beyond humiliated.

My uncle explained that I had suddenly fell face-first on the court, which explained all the clay and dirt on my knees and hands. I then noticed how my uncle couldn't stop staring at something on my face. Finally, I asked him what was the matter with my face? Somewhat shocked, he replied, "It's just amazing that you didn't break your nose. You literally fell facedown."

Once again, aside from a few minor scrapes, I had no serious injuries, and even though I was beginning to get extremely frustrated with my condition, I began thinking how it's a miracle that I'm still alive. I began to feel God's presence in my life, watching over me and protecting me. He was there with me, saying, "I know you're going through a rough season right now, but I'm here and we will get through it together."

My doctor and I decided to bump up the dose of the medication one more time, and if that didn't work, we would go back to my old medicine.

It was only a few months later that a third breakthrough seizure happened, and this time it was while I was shopping with my father. When I opened my eyes, lying on the floor of The Papery (a stationery store), looking up at my father's face, I knew. All the same feelings flooded back in an instant. Fear. Embarrassment. Shame. And a growing lack of confidence. It is such a weird feeling to not have control of your body or mind, knowing that at any given time it can control you. I think *that* is the beautiful lesson and reminder. I don't control my life, God does: I don't know my future, God does.

After this episode, I went back on my old medicine and the seizures started to be controlled again. I began to reflect on this experience. Why did all of this just happen? What was the purpose for me to go through all of this? Obviously, the first truth I learned is that I did not grow out of my condition. However, the more important realization was that the whole experience opened my heart. I had witnessed, first hand, my own personal miracles of God watching over me and making sure I was all right.

I believe I had to go through those tough times in order to relate to the many other epileptic patients out there, and also to stir the desire inside me to help bring more awareness to this life challenge. I believe God was using this difficult time to bring me closer to Him, to remind me that He is our creator and our God and, therefore, has a good plan for us. He reminded me that when times get tough, the tough go to God! We *need* Him!

Finally, this entire experience made me start to more greatly comprehend God's vast love for me. I say "start" because we can't fully comprehend the amount of love He has for each of us.

> *"And may you have the power to understand, as all God's people should, how wide, how long, how high, and how deep his love is. May you experience the love of Christ, though it is too great to understand fully"* (Ephesians 3:18-19 NLT).

I am imperfect, but He still loves me. In fact, He handpicked me and showed me how much He loves me by being with me every step of the way. My heart was forever awoken.

> **"Be strong and courageous. Do not be afraid; do not be discouraged, for the Lord your God will be with you wherever you go"** (Joshua 1:9 NIV).

FIRST STEPS

And I'll chase Your voice through the dark
Fix my eyes on the unexpected…so take another
step

—Hillsong United

"Be still, and know that I am God"
(Psalm 46:10 NIV).

This is the line that led me closer to the Lord, and also the reason why I have the letter *B* tattooed on my wrist.

It all started one night in 2014, when I was visiting with my in-laws. My mother-in-law Fran, who is a wonderful and inspirational Christ follower, and I were chatting late at night in their living room. At one point in our conversation, I noticed a small wooden sign above the television cabinet which read, "Be still and Know that I am God."

I had no idea what that line was from, and really didn't understand the true meaning or context behind it, so I became curious and asked her about the significance of that sign.

Little did I know that this little phrase and my simple question would stir up hours of conversation to come, and inevitably would lead to my salvation through Jesus Christ.

I will never forget her explanation. At times, in life, things feel like they are upside down and out of control, and it's during these times that she reminds herself to *be still*, give all her concerns and worries to God, and let Him take care of the things she can't. I loved that. I was so moved and intrigued by her words that I began to ask more questions.

The next few questions I asked were about God and Jesus, and heaven. I wanted to know more, but I didn't know where to start. So I chose the bigger topics that I knew a little bit about. I say "a little bit" because I grew up in the Catholic Church; going to Sunday school every week taught me the basics of Christianity, but I had never picked up or owned a Bible during my childhood. I knew about Jesus' birth, death, and resurrection, and that he performed many kinds of miracles, but my knowledge pretty much stopped there. It was basic. I believed in God, but I didn't know much about Him. He felt distant to me.

As I was talking to my mother-in-law, she was like a spring of knowledge and it was so refreshing to listen to her. She knew answers to my questions and quoted scripture verses while explaining things, and I quickly found myself wanting to obtain the same knowledge she knew. I gravitated toward the calm, loving, and spiritual glow that surrounded her. I wanted that for myself.

Near the end of our conversation, I remember her saying that, "It's not about how many times you go to church, or whether you memorize everything possible in the Bible (as though they were tasks on a to-do list), but it's everything about growing your relationship with God. That's what He wants most."

I was a little confused by this because I thought you had to always go to church in order to be close to God—wasn't that what made you a religious and good Christian? I quickly learned that wasn't necessarily true. She explained that going to church and reading the Bible will strengthen your relationship with God, as they are a wonderful form of worship and communication, but it's more about choosing to emulate Jesus on a daily basis through all that you do. This builds your character to be more *Christlike,* and as a result, you will love and serve others and most likely *want to* plug into a church with other Christ followers!

I asked, "How can I start?" I was hungry and anxious to know Jesus. I wanted the type of relationship she had with Him, and most importantly, I wanted to be part of God's family with her.

I think it was about two in the morning at that point, and she said to me, "You can start right now, it's so simple." She then asked me a couple of questions, "Do you believe in God?"

I immediately said, "Yes!"

Then she asked, "Do you believe that Jesus died for our sins?"

An immediate "Yes" again! That was it. It was so simple. She was right.

My mother-in-law shared with me that saying a small salvation prayer will open my heart to God and stir the Holy Spirit inside me. Without hesitation, we both stood up and I followed her into her office.

She opened the closet door in her office, which was stacked floor to ceiling with Christian books, and she scanned with her hand until she came to a tiny, thin book that she quickly grabbed out of the lineup. You could tell it was an old book as the spine was practically falling apart, and the book itself was a bright blue color that just read, *Power for Living.* No author's name, no subtext, no "New York Times Best Seller," nothing else.

She searched for the precise page she wanted, sixty-one, and told me to recite the prayer out loud. So I did.

"Dear God,

I've been living my life my own way. Now I want to live it your way. I need you and I am now willing for you to take control of my life. I receive your son Jesus Christ, as my personal Savior and Lord. I believe He died for my sins and has risen from the dead. I surrender to Him as Lord.

Come, Lord Jesus, and occupy the throne of my
life. Make me the kind of person you want me
to be."

As I read the prayer out loud, I could feel my heart beating
faster. Tears began to flow down my face. I felt as though a fire had
been lit inside me and my journey as a child of God had just started.
And it did.

When you say a powerful prayer like that, with true heartfelt
intentions, God hears you. He meets you, and that is where your
relationship grows. You can say that same prayer right now and watch
your relationship begin to blossom. I also highly recommend reading
Jamie Buckingham's book, *Power for Living*, especially if you are a
new Christian and just starting a relationship with God.

As one of my favorite authors Rick Warren says, the rest is "His-
story!" It's true, because ever since that night when I asked about
that special verse on the sign in her living room (which comes from
Psalm 46:10), my life has been changed, shifted, flipped, my old self
washed away, and a new life made with purpose.

I can't imagine it any other way.

WHO ARE YOU
BORN TO BE?

In my Father's house
There's a place for me
I'm a child of God
Yes I am.

—Hillsong United

I f you are someone who has witnessed a baby being born, or has had the experience of holding a newborn, it's pretty hard not to think that the whole process is nothing short of a miracle. It's amazing how a tiny little egg inside a woman grows into a small fetus, and then incubates for nine months until the baby is ready to be born. It's a miracle.

It is amazing to think how a woman's body instinctively knows how to adapt while carrying a baby, and knows how to nurture and feed it without her really even controlling the situation. It's a miracle.

Not only does this happen to millions of women on a daily basis, but this is only one example of the millions of miracles that occur every day.

There is only one place that miracles come from, and that is God. So if miracles are from God, and we were all at one-point newborn babies from our mother's womb, then we are in fact all God's children.

"God created man in His own image"
(Genesis 1:26–27 ESV)

When you look at a newborn baby, it's hard not to think how pure and innocent they are. How they have only had seconds in this world and have years of *unknown* experiences to come. It is almost a bit frightening and overwhelming to think about. A part of you may have a sudden urge to want to tuck that baby back inside its mother's belly to protect and shield it from that *unknown* world.

However, we can be relieved to know that every baby born into this world can have God as their shield and protector. He created us.

He is our true father standing in the delivery room and smiling over the new life he blessed the earth with.

Since we were made in His image, we have a place for His love, His forgiveness, and His Holy Spirit inside of us that is waiting to be filled. He wants us to love like He loves. He wants us to forgive like He forgives, and He wants us to choose to turn to Him through His Holy Spirit inside of us. The Holy Spirit is our signal, that "gut feeling," of always doing the right thing. God placed that feeling inside of us, and we must always pay attention to it. When you listen to it, you grow closer to God. You grow closer to your true Father.

God planned our entrance into this world. He planned who your parents are, He planned the timing and exact moment of your birth, and He planned everything about who you are. God also has a plan for your life. He has a plan for all the people you will meet, He has a plan for all the experiences you will go through, and He has a plan for everything that you will do.

God also has a plan for the way you will exit this earth. At first, this thought seems kind of daunting and dark to think about, because we like to be in control of our life and know everything that's going to happen, but the reality is that we can't. We are not in control of our lives and we do not know everything. But just as beautiful as birth is, death can be the same thing if you choose to live a life for God. A life following His image. A life of blessing others with your love, your forgiveness, and your character traits that reflect your true Father.

We were given life by God, so shouldn't we live life for Him? From the very moment on the clock that you entered this world, to the moment you leave, will you choose to live a life filled with your absolute best potential? A life depending on God, just as a newborn depends on their mother? Without the mother, that newborn would die. Similarly, without Jesus, we are dead inside. We are physically and spiritually unable to fulfill our purpose in life without Jesus.

Don't forget who you were born to be. Don't forget who gave you life. I have never had a child myself, but I do know where I came from and I do know who I am living for.

"Your eyes saw my unformed body; all the days ordained for me were written in your book before one of them came to be" (Psalm 139:16 NIV).

"For you are a mist that appears for a little time and then vanishes" (James 4:14 ESV).

YOU'RE INVITED!
HOW WILL YOU RSVP?

Come to the table

Come join the sinners who have been redeemed

Take your place beside the Savior

Sit down and be set free

Come to the table

—Sidewalk Prophets

This is one of my favorite songs and every time I hear that verse it stirs up my soul; it makes me smile and makes me want to get closer to God, more and more every day. It reminds me that being close with Him isn't hard. He did the hard part for us. All we need to do is to *accept* Him into our hearts and *choose* to develop a relationship with Him.

We can start our journey and grow our relationship with Him by talking to Him through prayer and relying on Him for guidance. God loves when we talk to Him and our conversations can be simple. We can talk to Him literally anytime we want (i.e., in the car, doing chores around the house, at work, etc.) because He is always there. I used to think that prayer was something that always had to be formal and required a certain posture, but it doesn't. It is simply our thoughts and heart talking to God.

We can continue to build our relationship with Him, by giving Him thanks for everything we have and every piece of who we are. I always remind myself that for every hard time I experience, there is something positive to be learned. I just may not see it yet. Giving thanks changes my perspective regarding a negative situation and is a discipline that reminds me that there is always something to be thankful for.

To continue our growth with God, we need to trust in Him and obey His Word, even when times are tough or things aren't going exactly as we planned. It's sometimes a difficult thing to do, but we must keep our eyes focused on Him, and know His plan is the right one for us.

It actually sounds like all He wants is for us to let Him in, and for us to be His friend so that He can be our truest companion. Is that something you want? I know I do. I also know that as much as *we say* it's not hard to do these things, *we do* find it hard to remain focused and give God the time and energy he deserves each day.

We get distracted so easily every day, and technology doesn't help. If we don't plug "God time" into our daily routine, then it's too easy to say, "Oh, I'll get back on schedule tomorrow." Then "tomorrow" turns into five days gone by and other things have gotten in the way of time with Him. Giving Him less and less of ourselves when He deserves every piece of us.

Every day is an invitation. Every day is a new gift. We shouldn't live in the past because we can't change it. We can't live for those hypothetical and unknown situations that the future *may* or *may not* hold, a life of worry, because we don't know the future. All we can do is live in this present day. We *can* make the best decisions given the wisdom and knowledge we have, keeping God at the center of it all. We *can* focus on being the best "me" we can possibly be each day.

We *can* leave our sin and shame at the door and accept God's invitation to join Him each day. He forgives us for our failures, flaws, negative behavior and sins of all kinds. In fact, he forgives *you* and is waiting for *you* to come and sit beside Him, to be His best friend, to confide in Him, and to go to Him when you need help or reassurance. He is there for you, and each day a new invitation awaits. No one is excluded from the guest list.

When I am feeling far from God, because I haven't been giving Him the time he deserves of me each day, I remember that the invitation to join Him and sit in His presence is always open. It's not a question of being invited or not, but rather a question of how I RSVP.

35

Are you staring at the invite and debating what to do, instead of just accepting and seeing what happens? Are you saying, "I'll respond later," while tossing it on the counter because you're distracted with a million other things at the moment? Maybe you just don't have time? Are you not making time because He is such a good friend and will understand and will always forgive you? I mean, if he's not going to be mad, then it's not really that big of a deal, right?

Or maybe you respond yes because you are looking forward to the time together. Maybe you understand that there is nothing whatsoever to lose by accepting the invitation.

Whatever your response is, it's important to understand that *the way* you respond is a direct reflection of you. It reflects how you are as a friend. Don't you want to be a good friend? Someone who is loyal, trustworthy, committed, kind and positive? Don't you think Jesus deserves that type of friendship from you? Especially after He gave His life for you? He gets it! He knows we are not perfect, He knows we were born sinners and will continually make mistakes, but He also knows that we *need Him*!

Therefore, every day when you wake up, you need to know that a beautiful invitation awaits you, hand addressed with your name written in the most perfect calligraphy. The invitation is being outstretched to you by your eternal and truest companion in life.

Will you take it? How will you RSVP?

"Behold, I stand at the door and knock, If anyone hears my voice and opens the door, I will come in." Rev. 3:20

THAT BOOK CALLED
THE BIBLE

There is a new song in my soul
And it begins when I breathe in
Your word of life

—Jeremy Camp

What's that book all about anyway?

I feel like so many people are nervous or cautious to say the word "Bible" out loud. They are resistant because they don't want the negative judgements that society has associated with the Bible. Those judgements that a person who reads the Bible is "super religious" or "closed minded" or lives an "abnormal life." In reality, I feel like the Bible is intimidating to many people because they don't really know what it's all about!

Often times in life, when we don't know someone very well we may be skeptical about them. We try different angles of evaluating the person (based on our own opinions and assumptions) without really giving them a fair chance to show their true self to us. Sometimes if we have heard something negative about someone, or if someone says something that's a little insulting to us, then we distance ourselves from them. At times, we will even resist and avoid conversing or becoming friends with someone who seems like a *potential* threat to us. Those people that may be better than us at a sport, or a work colleague who is aiming for that same promotion spot. We often will do everything possible to avoid that person because of the potential *unknown* or *threat* they can be to us.

Can you relate to any of these behaviors? I can, because I have been there and felt this way before. I find it interesting to reflect on this, because I feel like this is the type of behavior we display toward the Bible. Some people may not know much about it (the scriptures, life lessons, etc.) so they develop their own opinions and assumptions on what it's about without ever reading it.

Some people may have heard things about the Bible through other people. They live their life based on what others think and say, and as a result, distance themselves from ever reading it.

Others may avoid it completely because they see it as a potential threat to their current lifestyle. They think their life is good and resist the concept of being told how to live.

The truth is, the Bible *will* challenge you to change and live a life totally driven to *be* the person that God made you to be. God's plan is independent from *your plan* for your life. The truth is, you think you know who you were born to be, but you have no clue without the guidance from God's Word, the Bible.

It's common for us to resist being told what to do. Even from the time we were children, we didn't like our parents telling us what to do. We want things our own way. So when we hear friends talking about the Bible and the way we *should* be living our lives, we often don't want to hear it. It is easier to avoid the Bible and tune out its message.

If there is ever anything that may even remotely seem more powerful or better than us, we tend to feel immediately threatened by it. Remember that kid on your sports team that was just a little bit better than you? The one who you avoided and developed opinions about, that most likely were not true.

We judge. We all know judging isn't fair or nice, but we all have done it, whether it has been verbal or thought based, it's a judgement passed.

I feel as though many people judge the Bible before ever opening it and giving it a fair chance. They have their own opinions and assumptions about it without ever really taking the time to read it! I believe that the Bible is the only book on this planet that teaches us how we can all learn to be a better person and live our best lives.

The Bible is a book for all ages and all people. Whether it's a story I'm reading about Jesus in the New Testament or about a prophet in the Old Testament, I can't help but imagine myself back in time with them. I envision what is taking place around them, I learn about the people they encounter, and learn from the guidance these key figures passed through to my generation. I'm fascinated by the miracles that were conducted and the power of belief and prayer; it's all so inspiring and addicting to read.

The Bible also outlines the mistakes people have made in the past, and the repercussions they paid as a result of their sin and evil behavior. It speaks of the times that people angered God and how there were times they lived far away and distant from Him spiritually.

There are so many great things about reading the Bible, but the best thing about it is that the author is right there reading along with you. God's Word speaks differently and purposefully to every single heart reading it. I don't know of any other book in the world that does that!

His Word is life.

The Bible is a living book.

What is it saying to you?

ELIJAH, EVER HEARD OF HIM?

The real miracle of Elijah's life was his very personal relationship with God. And that same miracle is available to us!

—Life Application Study Bible (NLT)

E lijah is pretty much one of the coolest guys I've ever heard of. He was a person who wholeheartedly loved the Lord. He conducted many miracles that we talk about today, and what I love most is that Elijah's power is within us too.

> *"All that happened in Elijah's life began with the same miracle that is available to us—he responded to the miracle of being able to know God"* (Life Application Study Bible, NLT).

I have noticed a common theme that runs throughout my writings—the importance of building a relationship with God. Your relationship with Him is where your real life begins here on earth. I want true life, a true relationship with God, and the way to do it is to do exactly what Elijah did. *"He responded."* Those are the two most powerful words from the quote.

He was invited to know God on a personal level, and so are we! The question is, how are you responding? Are you open and ready to receive and nurture that miracle that sits inside you?

If you responded yes to this question not only verbally but wholeheartedly, and choose to develop a more intimate relationship with God each day, then your awareness of His presence all around you will become magnified. You will begin to see the world in a new light. Praising and worshiping Him more and more each day will become a new form of life. Glorifying Him through all that you do will instill happiness and reading His Word and living by His doctrine will allow God to begin to work through you.

Relationship building and spiritual growth are tightly knit together. One important aspect that they share is time. It takes time to get to know someone and grow your relationship with them, just as it takes time to increase your spiritual knowledge, practice, and character. Our society loves immediate gratification (I know I do), but I have learned that time and patience are required for proper spiritual growth.

If you accept the invitation to grow a relationship with God and surrender to Him daily, like Elijah did, then there is no limit to what God can do through you.

Elijah performed many miracles, or better said, God worked many miracles through Elijah, who 100 percent committed his life to God.

"The God I serve" (1 Kings 17:1 NLT).

Elijah never questioned God's requests or commands, and he always trusted in the timing of God's plan.

As a result of his unbreakable faith, God used Elijah to bring a dead child back to life. God enabled Elijah to provide endless food to a starving widow during a time of tremendous drought when crops didn't grow for several years. And He selected Elijah to represent Him in a showdown with priests and prophets who betrayed God and believed in false gods.

That last miracle I mentioned, the showdown, is my favorite. It demonstrates the intimate and awesome connection that Elijah and God shared. That type of relationship which is inspiring, admirable, and truthfully, is one that I want to have with God too.

In this story, Elijah challenged more than eight hundred people who were following false gods and worshiping wooden statues, columns, and golden calves to try to prove that their gods were more powerful than our Lord Almighty. Everyone gathered on Mount Carmel, and Elijah instructed the people to prepare a bull to be sacrificed on two altars, one on theirs and one on his.

After both altars were set up, Elijah made a deal with the head guy, Ahab, representing all the people. He said that the two of them would call upon their respective deities. Whichever one brought fire to the altar would be recognized as the one true God by all.

As the excitement, tension, and silence was building, Elijah asked for the people to stack wood all over his altar and then pour buckets of water all over the wood. I love that part. I love how his faith in God was so strong and unwavering that he had the fuel saturated in water, so when the truth was revealed, the people could not waver in knowing that his God was the one and only true God!

I could imagine how the people and prophets of the false gods who prayed, shouted, and danced all day for the fire to ignite on their altar were sorely disappointed when nothing happened. I'm sure tempers were aroused, and anger and frustration filled the air.

Then it was Elijah's turn. By himself. The only *one* of the eight hundred people representing God.

He went up to his altar, dug into the depths of his heart, and prayed hard.

> *"O Lord, answer me! Answer me so these
> people will know that you, O Lord, are God"*
> (1 Kings 18:37 NLT).

Immediately, the blazing fire came down from the sky and burned Elijah's altar to dust, waterlogged wood and all!

Envisioning this scene not only makes me literally cheer on Elijah, but also puts a smile across my face and brings goosebumps to my skin. Why? Because I know that this same power lives in me!

No matter the *scale* of a miracle, God can use you every day to perform them, just like He did with Elijah.

When you live a life dedicated to growing your relationship with God, then there is no limit to how much power the Holy Spirit inside of you can be channeled.

We are meant *for* big things, and meant to *do* big things, but it all starts with believing *BIG*!

ARE YOU A BACK SEAT DRIVER?

Jesus, take the wheel
Take it from my hands
'Cause I can't do this on my own
I'm letting go

—Carrie Underwood

If Jesus was driving and you were in the passenger seat, would you tell Him where to go? Would you question His turns or speed? Would you feel unsafe and grab the door handle for dear life? I know I wouldn't. In fact, if Jesus was behind the wheel of my car, I would feel completely comfortable falling asleep, knowing and trusting that He knows where we're going.

Every day, I pray that Jesus will take the wheel of my life and show me what He needs me to do.

For a while, I used to struggle with the concept and question of what my purpose is in life. For some people, their purpose is crystal clear. For example, my dear friend Christian Andrews, is an incredible pastor, and when you hear him preach God's Word you say to yourself, "Wow, he was born to do that!" Do you have a friend that is such a doting, loving, caring mother that when you see her in "mom mode," you think, "Wow, she makes it look so easy! Her purpose in life is definitely to be a mom"?

There are many people that seem to have a clear purpose, but I felt that I didn't know mine!

My husband, for example, is a very well-respected speaker and trainer in the digital marketing world and he loves every minute of what he does. He loves teaching others, helping them understand new strategies, inspiring them to be better, and opening up opportunities where he sees that they can grow. I have never seen him give less than a perfect speech. He always connects with his audience, and after his presentations are over, at least half of the room lines up to speak with him. It's actually very inspiring to watch as his wife, I smile knowing that he is in "his element" and he is serving his purpose.

Watching him do what he does on a regular basis with such a clear-cut path in his life made me reflect on my path. It made me ask myself, "What is my purpose?" I realized—thanks to my favorite book, *The Purpose Driven Life* by Rick Warren—that I didn't have the answer. I kept digging and digging inside of myself and reflecting. I asked the question, "What do I want to do with my life?" But it's not up to me. I can't see or predict my future, so how can I tell myself what to be? I can't, but God can. He sees the entire road ahead, and guess what? He's the driver! He's behind the wheel choosing the direction to take, not me!

The only way for me to figure out my purpose is through Jesus, by developing a close relationship with Him and reading His Word daily. I have also accepted the idea that I may not ever know my life-long purpose, but I do know that I will impact people every day of my life, which will contribute to the larger purpose God has for the world. I know that I am part of His plan.

What can I do every day until I find that clear purpose? I can focus on being the best passenger possible. I can listen to Him while He is driving; I can talk to Him about my thoughts and problems. I can laugh and thank Him for the wonderful times.

There will always be speed bumps, detours, and "not-so-smooth sailing," but through it all there is Jesus. Let Him take the wheel!

BEST FRIENDS

God has no phone, but I talk to Him.

He has no Facebook but he is still my friend.

He does not have Twitter but I still follow Him.

—Anonymous

God wants nothing more than to be best friends with you. He wants to be the person you go to for sharing great news, sorrow, excitement, pain, joy, thankfulness - everything. He wants you to include Him through it all! Even though He is an ever-present God, He is not going to *make* you be friends with Him. He wants you to *choose* to be friends with Him. He wants your heart to accept Him into your life. After all, is it really true friendship if you force someone to be friends with you?

Sometimes life gets busy, or as many say, we experience a "busy season in life," and we may start to grow a little distant from God. We may stop finding time to go to church, or procrastinate reading our Bible every day, or we don't pray or talk to God as much throughout our day. And many times, we may find It difficult to just *be still* in silence with God. We just have too many other things to do, or we say "God will understand." Can you imagine what would happen if you treated a human friend like that and then expected them to always be there for you? It just wouldn't fly. Eventually, you would lose that person as a friend. Even though God *is* always there for us, is it really fair of us to treat Him that way?

Taking time to *be still* and present for a few minutes each day is a difficult task that requires much discipline, particularly in our day and age. Not only for people like myself who consider themselves to be an active person and always "on-the-go," but it's also difficult because of all the technology and distractions that surround us. I have found that if I don't take time to *be still* and present with God first thing in the morning, then it often escapes from me during the day. Especially when I travel in and out of different time zones, in a sleep-deprived state, I feel it hardest to wake up early in the morning and *be still* with God. My body is telling me "sleep" and my heart is telling me "make space for God time." It's so easy for me to say to myself, "I'll do it tomorrow" or "God will understand."

However, it's struggles like this that remind me how the distancing between a person and God can quickly begin. It starts with one excuse or point of procrastination and develops into a habit over time. It's moments like this that snap me back into prioritizing my day the right way.

Every morning when I take time to pray, read my devotional books, read my Bible, and write my thoughts and reflections in my journal, I feel whole. I feel at peace, I feel secure with who I am and who I am living for. I feel as though I can take on the day, spiritually armed with the confidence and perspective that I need.

God doesn't deserve anything less than all of us. He knows that we will always fall short of perfection, but He still loves us. He still wants to be our best friend and companion for life, our secret keeper and King above all kings.

I recently wrote an "intimacy" prayer asking for God to speak to me. Not to speak to me about a specific thing or topic, but just to communicate with me on a deeper level. A request-prayer like this is pleasing to God, and even if He doesn't respond right away, I know He hears my prayer and smiles knowing that I want to draw closer to Him.

However, I also know that God often speaks in different ways, meaning it's not always through conversation that He speaks. Sometimes He uses music, books, people, or scripture. I prayed that my heart, mind, ears, and eyes will always be open and aware when God speaks.

Here is the prayer that I wrote and pray daily. Feel free to use it as your prayer as well:

Dear God,

I want to know Your voice like a sheep knows its shepherd's voice. I want to have an intimate relationship with You in addition to living by Your Word. Please open my eyes, ears, and heart to hear the small and big ways that You speak to me, because I don't want to miss anything.

Anytime of the day or night I will be ready and waiting for You.

Meet me, God, meet me here.

Amen.

I prayed that prayer by saying each line slowly out loud, and then reflected on it one line at a time. Afterward, I closed my eyes and meditated on the phrase, "Speak to me, tell me what you want me to hear." While saying this one line over and over to myself, I realized it was one of the first times that no other thoughts were trying to distract me. I felt still in God's presence. That phrase was the only thing I could think of, when suddenly the word "space" came into my mind. My eyes shot open and I started wondering why. *Why space? Space what?* Then it transformed into "create space." I started to meditate on that while grabbing a pen and paper to further explore my thoughts.

As I began writing what that phrase meant to me, it was clear that I felt like God was asking for me to create more space for Him.

This made complete sense to me, not only because my days are busy, but if I don't set aside time in my schedule I can overlook things. Furthermore, who can develop a relationship with someone without *creating space* for that person in their life? You can't. You won't be able to get to know that person's personality, talents, life stories, or voice if you don't spend time and talk with them.

I want to know God's voice like I know my husband's, instinctively. When my husband Brian talks or whispers to me, I immediately know his voice. That's how I want to know God's voice. I want to instinctively know all the ways he speaks to me, so that I never miss one moment.

"Be still, and know that I am God"
(Psalm 46:10 NIV).

UNFINISHED

No, my God's not done making me a masterpiece
He's still working on me
He started something good and I'm gonna believe it
He started something good and He's gonna complete it
So I'll celebrate the truth, His work in me ain't through
I'm just unfinished

—Mandisa

I am so grateful for all the wonderful travel experiences God has blessed me and my husband with, as I love seeing all the different parts of His world. I love learning about new cultures, exploring new territories, and speaking new languages. I am specifically grateful for the deep love God has planted inside of me for the country of Italy. Not only did I love the country when I first studied abroad in Florence during college, but He knew that my lifelong partner and husband, Brian Pasch, shared the same love for Italy and would bring out that passion of mine, making it shine even more.

He knew we would be the best travel companions, that we shared the same impulsive excitement to buy a ticket with our saved miles to jet across the world—Paris, Italy, London, Prague, Holland, Greece—to simply *live* in the moment together. My husband and I are compatible in so many ways, and this was one of the first things we learned and loved about each other, which is our passion for traveling together.

What is so awesome for me to think about is how God's plan for me falling even more in love with Italy was also through Brian and me discovering his family in Popoli (a small village in the Abruzzo region of Italy).

A few years ago, we took on the project of researching Brian's family tree. This entailed spending extensive hours on Ancestry.com, and during the midst of our dig, we found ourselves missing some key lineage gaps. We needed help. So Brian decided to post a portrait of his family from the early 1900s on Facebook, to see if anyone in Popoli could help identify a few of the people in the photo. Oddly enough, a few hours later, a cousin from Popoli (whom we had never met before and, by the grace of God, spoke English) responded to his post. One Facebook message led to another, and another, and a virtual friendship was born. It wasn't long before Brian and I looked at each other, and immediately began checking ticket prices and the soonest possible dates that we could fly to Popoli to meet them.

From that first visit, over five years ago, Brian and I have visited our family in Popoli over a few dozen times. We got married in Italy just a few minutes away from Popoli, we created a charity to help the local school system build a new music department in Brian's grandfather's honor, and I had the pleasure of working in our cousin's café to help practice my Italian. So many new experiences were birthed from this one Facebook post, which is sometimes overwhelming to think about. But that's exactly how God works—in abundance!

Through this all, I have made some of the most special friendships with people I will treasure forever. My friends and family in Popoli have since opened their doors to me and assured me that I always have a home there. I love them so much and always want to visit them.

Life in Popoli is so different than life in the United States. It's so simple compared to the millions of distractions we have here on a daily basis. I always leave there feeling relaxed, recharged, and focused on the beauties of life, the beauties that God gave us from day one—each other (family, friends, and neighbors). We can't lose sight of our lasting legacy on this earth, our relationships. We must focus on building each other up and loving each other, because in the end, that is the only thing we will leave behind.

Over the years of traveling to Italy, I have learned to speak the Italian language pretty fluently. I say "pretty fluently" because I always ask myself, "Is one ever truly fluent in a language?" There are plenty of English words that I don't know, so learning a language is a lifelong journey. This is why I continue to take Italian lessons via Skype three times a week with my Italian teacher, who lives in Florence. There is still so much more for me to learn! It's become a lifelong passion of mine that God has motivated me to pursue, and I love it!

With that said, there have been two monumental moments thus far that made me smile and say, "This is awesome, I'm really doing it!"

The first experience where I felt completely comfortable with my fluency in the Italian language was in August 2017, when my husband and I lived in Florence for five weeks so I could attend a private school to help "push me over the edge" into fluency. I originally was only going to do three-hour, one-on-one sessions (fluent Italian) per day. However, after my first day, I returned to our apartment and Brian asked me how it went. Without hesitation, I told him that I wanted to add more hours. I think he thought that maybe it was too easy for me, and to a degree he was right, but it was really because I was doing it! I was in the process of achieving my goal. I could literally feel my brain clicking and saying, "Yes! You got it!"

My teacher was excellent and I ended up doing six hours per day for five weeks. To be able to talk to someone in Italian for six hours a day was a huge accomplishment for me.

The second experience that reinforced my knowledge of the language and my deep desire to become fluent was in September 2017.

In September 2017, my two sweet friends from Popoli, Erika and Lia, wanted to come visit us in America. They had never been on a plane before and didn't speak a lick of English. Of course, I didn't even think before telling them, "Of course! You must come!" I wanted them to stay with us and share our daily experiences with them!

I wanted them to feel the same way I do about Popoli—that my door is always open to them!

However, stepping back for one moment, you should know that Brian and I have had the privilege of hosting our cousin Luca and his son Jacopo a few times over the years here in the States. Throughout their visits, Brian and I showed them New York, Florida, Tennessee, Washington, DC, and Philadelphia. We feel truly blessed to have met such great people, and to have had the ability to entertain them and show them these different parts of our country. Also, traveling with them was never a problem because they both spoke English.

So getting back to my two friends Erika and Lia. As the date approached, I could tell they were getting very nervous. They were asking a million travel questions because they had never traveled on such a trip before, but they were also experiencing the natural "language barrier" anxieties. "How will I order off menus? How will I buy stuff in stores? How will I ask for directions?"

From the moment I picked them up at the airport, I was not only speaking Italian with them but also translating for them. I was doing double duty asking waitstaff, salespeople, etc., questions on their behalf, plus trying to practice and speak as much as possible for my own benefit. Let's just say that my brain was thinking, dreaming, and translating Italian 24-7!

The best part of their entire visit wasn't only the laughs we shared or the practice I received, but the fact that I was able to break down the wall of anxiety they had. I was able to eliminate the language barrier entirely. They would not have been able to take that trip without me, and that was an especially rewarding feeling.

I love thinking about these stories and experiences not only because they were fun and I was achieving something awesome, but because I could literally feel God working inside me. I could feel Him using the seed he planted in my heart to learn the beautiful Italian language for some larger purpose. I could hear Him saying, "Carrie, I gave you this passion for Italian and all your hard work and knowledge for moments like this in helping others."

This story is kind of an open-ended story for me, because I know God has so much more in store for me with my Italian. I am not exactly sure why I was given this passion in my heart to learn the language, or what the future holds with it, but I know that there is a reason behind it. It's exciting to know that I am a work in progress and that God uses every ounce of me for a bigger purpose.

We all have different things that we are passionate about, and since that is something that makes each of us unique, God wants us to use them as ways to serve Him and others. How can we use our passions to connect with others and more importantly, with God?

I know there is a reason that I will be serving God with my Italian in the future—"His work in me ain't through, I'm just unfinished."

GIVE GOD ALL YOU GOT

Whatever you do, work at it with all your heart,
as working for the Lord, not for men.

—Colossians 3:23

God created each one of us uniquely. No one is the same, which is a miracle in itself. Not only is our physical makeup different, but our character traits and personalities are different too. Think about all those different combinations! That is why it's so hard for me to hear how people don't believe that God loves and cares for each and every one of us individually. God confirms this by the beautiful scripture verse found in the Book of Jeremiah stating, *"I knew you before I formed you in your mother's womb. Before you were born I set you apart"* (Jeremiah 1:5 NLT).

He knows us better then we know ourselves, because He made us!

"You understand my every thought before it even enters my mind. You are so intimately aware of me, Lord. You read my heart like an open book and You know all the words I'm about to speak before I even start a sentence!" (Psalm 139:2–4 TPT).

If we want to live our best lives and find our true purpose in life, then we must consult and lean on the One who created us and knows us best! We won't be able to find "life's purpose" by searching deep inside ourselves because we only know what we know, and God created us to depend on Him.

New York Times Bestselling Author Rick Warren explains this concept so perfectly in his book, *The Purpose Driven Life: What on Earth Am I Here For* by saying:

"If I handed you an invention you had never seen before, you wouldn't know its purpose, and the invention itself wouldn't be able to tell you either. Only the creator or the owner's manual could reveal its purpose."

Obviously, our creator is God and the owner's manual is His Word (the Bible). He knows every detail of your past and future. He knows what career path you're going to take, what kind of family life you're going to have, where you're going to live, what mistakes you're going to make—everything. Wouldn't it be silly to know that God holds all this information and not go to Him for everything? For example, if you are deciding on what career path to take, are you consulting friends, books, a therapist, or God? When you find the desire to start a family, are you comparing yourself to other friends who have children, getting frustrated and stressed, or consulting God on your path for a family?

My point is, He is always there. He is omnipresent in your life and He knows all, so why aren't you including Him in everything?

Depending on God and reading His Word will make your purpose crystal clear, day by day.

With that said, we as humans can only function at a certain level of efficiency without God. If we don't accept Him, thank Him, depend on Him, and glorify Him through all that we do, then we are similar to a toy without batteries, or a car without gas—they are nice to look at, play with, and even function on a basic level, but when paired with a full charge or a filled fuel tank, they can run at their most efficient and productive level.

Don't you want to be the most productive and best you that you can possibly be? I do! We need God to do that! Every day, I remind myself *how* and *why* I am here, and I give thanks to God through all I do.

MEDITATION OF THE HEART

A PERSONAL JOURNAL ENTRY TO JESUS

Dear Jesus,

Thank you for this beautiful snowy day here in New Jersey. The silence outside combined with everything glazed over with Your fine powdery flakes is so peaceful and it reminds me of Your powerful presence. I love the snow.

It's amazing how the smallest pile of snow can sit on the tiniest leaf or twig without it bending or breaking.

It's amazing how the wind creates a playground of drifts across the backyard and around the house—no single one the same height, depth, or shape.

It's amazing how the squirrels, birds, and wildlife adapt to the weather and can survive the cold temperature.

It's amazing how the snowstorms bring the beauty of the wind. You can see and feel the swirling clouds of white flakes around you, and see the waves of white blow over the roofs of houses. It's one of the few times you can actually *see* the wind.

On an average day, wind is something we can't necessarily see or even feel, but we know it's there. One day, the wind may be howling and another it may be perfectly still. Either way, it's always there. Like You, Jesus. We need the air in order to breathe and we need You in order to live.

When the snow is swirling, when everything is covered in white, when nature is silent, Your presence is more abundant than ever.

I see Your beauty all around me.

SPIRITUALLY TRAINED

You see right through the mess inside me
And you call me out to pull me in…
I'm fully known and loved by You
You won't let go no matter what I do

—Tauren Wells

I am so grateful for my health and daily motivation to work out each day. It's interesting because this past year was a very trying one for me in terms of health. I found out that there are parts of my body internally that can't function to the best of their ability, and therefore, would make it extremely difficult for me to carry a child full term.

However, I feel the most in shape and healthiest than I ever have before. Going through this recent experience, and also having epilepsy since I was two years old, reminds me how we all have pieces and parts of our bodies that are broken and not perfect, but they shouldn't stop us from being the best we can be. In fact, I see them as opportunities to make me stronger, to trust in God, and have faith in Him that He believes in me and has a specific plan for each of us.

I could sit here and focus on all the negative aspects of my previous health experiences, or I can be confident and know that God will never give me anything I can't handle. He knows my weaknesses and He knows my strengths. He knows that working out each day and making smart food choices is important to me. He knows it makes me feel strong and healthy, even though I know my body isn't perfect. He gives me the strength I need to get through each day. More importantly, He gives me the strength I need to best serve Him.

When I am not at my best physically, then I don't feel great about myself and I start thinking how God deserves the best of me, nothing less. How can I be the best me when I don't put my health first? The answer is, I can't.

I have observed that being healthy and being children of God are similar in more ways than one. As children of God, we sometimes find ourselves going to church for habitual reasons, rather than being driven by the Spirit inside us to be there. Maybe we are the kind of children of God that love seeing people give and serve, but find it difficult to get out of our daily routine to go out and serve others. We get stuck in our own self-serving habits. Similarly, humans naturally become envious or resentful towards how other people look. Our first instinct is to focus on our physical imperfections rather than taking action, and focusing on being the best we can be with what God has given us. We often let our pride get in the way or resort to ways of self-doubt and insecurity. All of these paths and thoughts draw us apart from God.

As children of God, we catch ourselves complaining about aspects of church or community groups, or we judge and criticize others. The same goes for our health choices. It's so much easier to complain about the gym or make excuses to not do some sort of aerobic movement each day. Our minds try to trick us by saying, "You don't need to do it today. Take the day off. You don't need to go to Church to volunteer today, plenty of other people will be there. You do enough." But that's exactly it! We must constantly retrain our brains from this negative thinking. You are part of a bigger picture! You matter!

As my local lead pastor of Christ Fellowship Church, Todd Mullins, once said, "Remove the stinkin' thinkin'."

As we can see, these two life paths, being children of God and leading a healthy lifestyle, are not necessarily easy paths, but they are the right ones. They aren't always the popular or glamorous roads, but they will make you the strongest and healthiest person you can be, physically and spiritually.

Each day, I give thanks to God that He has given me the motivation and physical ability to work out, stay fit, and be healthy. I am

His. Who am I to treat my body with unhealthy practices? Wouldn't that be taking things for granted and disrespecting our creator?

Each day, I work out for God. When I am exercising, I thank Him and talk to Him because working out for myself is never truly a hundred-percent fulfilling. Working out for God is so much better! It gives purpose, motivation, and lifelong endurance to every work-out I do; it's the best exercise program of my life!

> *"And whatever you do, in word or deed, do everything in the name of the Lord Jesus, giving thanks to God the Father through him" (Colossians 3:17 ESV).*

HAPPY BIRTHDAY JESUS

You were the Word at the beginning
One with God the Lord Most High
Your hidden glory in creation
Now revealed in You our Christ
What a beautiful Name it is
What a beautiful Name it is
The Name of Jesus Christ my King
                    —Hillsong Worship

Today is a day we dedicate to giving. Giving love, giving kindness, and let's not forget giving presents. Today is a day that many people who normally function on high-stress mode or rarely spend time with their family, or even scarcely show a smile, begin to let down their guard a bit. It is a season where many cautiously embrace gratefulness, love, and sympathy to others.

Today is also a day that we praise the Good Lord for the birth of His Son, Jesus. Through Him, we have been given a human example of how to best live our own lives, and most importantly, we have been given a Savior who's set us free from our sins and has deposited a piece of himself in us that guarantees us everlasting life.

December 25th is the best and happiest day of the year for many, but my question is, why don't we live *every day* like this? Why don't we celebrate Christmas *every day*? Why don't we show love, kindness, sympathy, gratitude, and generosity toward one another always? Wouldn't that be following Jesus' example? Why don't we praise God *every day* for the birth of His Son who washes us clean from sin? Why do many of us only reserve one day a year to practice these wonderful things?

When we put into practice these human acts toward others, we are glorifying God. He sees it. He made us to be that way, and every time we show love, generosity, gratefulness, and praise Him, He smiles! He is the proud father saying, "That a girl! Go, be the person I taught you to be!"

It's through these moments that you feel closest to God, as though you are being the best *you* that you can be. It's also through these moments that you shine in the eyes of others. People notice the lightness, the peacefulness and the love you're speaking, and it becomes contagious. They want to obtain that level of happiness too and often start changing themselves. They start letting the light in little by little.

All this is the work of God in you, spreading the news ever so gently and kindly. You're a light in the darkness and you're being who you were made to be.

Many of us are familiar with the phrase, "Spreading Christmas Cheer." In fact, this phrase is often described with some of the same words I used before: happiness, kindness, generosity, love, and almost every other positive word you can think of. So my challenge to you is to be more *Christlike* and spread *CHRISTmas cheer* every day, just like you do on Christmas Day!

> *"The Word became flesh and made his dwelling among us. We have seen his glory, the glory of the one and only Son, who came from the Father, full of grace and truth" (John 1:14 NIV).*

F-R-I-E-N-D-S

It is the Holy Spirit's job to convict.
God's job to judge
and my job to love.

—Billy Graham

I am truly grateful for all the people God has instrumentally placed in my life. Some for a reason, some for a season, and some for a lifetime.

I am grateful that He is teaching me not to judge others. I say teaching rather than taught, because judging is a default thing we do as humans. Therefore, every day we must *choose* to retrain our brain and practice the act of not judging others. Ultimately, we will all be judged when we meet Him in Heaven, so who are we to take it upon ourselves to judge others? Wouldn't we be proclaiming to be wiser than God if He is the Judge above all judges, yet we think that we have the right to have a judgement on everything?

I have learned to accept people for who they are instead of who I expect them to be. If their friendship is negative or nonreciprocal, then I peacefully move on. I choose this path rather than judging, getting disappointed, and remaining friends with them, which only makes that circle go around and around.

I had to learn this lesson through many trials and tribulations over the years. There were times when I was made fun of as a young girl, bullied, or taken advantage of by a friend. I often found myself saying, "But how could she do that to me after everything I have done for her?" I often was disappointed by my friends and frequently hurt.

My problem was that I kept going back to them. I would repeat my mistakes by seeking their friendship and allowing them to bring me down. I see now that I had to go through these difficult years because it has made me a stronger person today. These experiences have also sharpened my perspective on building and accepting friendships.

You should always give your honest heart to friends through love, loyalty, and compassion, but when you feel that the person never seems to reciprocate those things back to you, then maybe it's time to evaluate if the friendship is worth your time and energy. True friendship doesn't require analysis.

Instead of judging or hating the person for the qualities they lack, I simply remind myself that they are who they are. They only know how to be that person, unless they decide to change. Therefore, I must accept them for that and move on!

Having this perspective releases our natural human habit of judging people, and forces us to have a more positive and accepting attitude toward others.

Do I hold feelings of anger, hatred, and regret toward the friends I grew up with? Friends that made me sit by myself at lunch in high school or called to tell me that I wasn't invited to a party or sent mean emails to me? No, I don't. In fact, I want to take this opportunity to thank them. They taught me a great deal about the different levels of friendships in life, and as I started to defend myself to them, my confidence grew.

I would say that today, confidence is an attribution of mine and I couldn't have achieved that without those experiences. Having to deal with many not-so-true friends over the years has made me be very in tune to others and myself.

I am constantly evaluating myself as a friend, and I know there are always ways to improve. As a result, I truly adore and love the close friends that I have. The ones I can pick up within five minutes after not seeing each other for a while. The ones who are always there for me no matter what decisions I make. The ones who laugh and cry with me and, most importantly, the ones that know my true heart. Solid friendships are hard to find and are a blessing. They take work, time, and energy, but so does every positive relationship in life. If everything was easy and required no work or effort, wouldn't we be aimless, wandering around all day with no purpose, no challenges to make us better, no individual traits to contribute to one another?

Instead, we are all lights. We need to share our light to serve others, exchanging and borrowing from each other as we move through life.

We must remember that God made us individually different, unique lights. We need each other because He made us to go through life together, not alone. We must remember one of the most important of life's commandments, *"love your neighbor as yourself"* (Mark 12:31 NIV).

"In the same way, let your light shine before others, so that they may see your good works and give glory to your Father who is in heaven" (Matthew 5:16 ESV).

PERSISTENCE IN PRAYER

I know if You wanted to You could wave Your hand
Spare me this heartache, and change Your plan
And I know any second You could take my pain
away
But even if You don't, I pray

—Natalie Grant

One of my personality traits is persistence. When I focus my mind on something, I don't stop until I get it. When I have a specific vision for one of the events that I organize for work, which requires x amount of sponsorship dollars and y amount of attendees, speakers, space, etc., I don't stop until the goal is achieved.

When I first committed myself to learning Italian four years ago, I started working with my cousin from Milan. He tutored me three times each week over Skype, regardless of what time zone I was in due to my intense travel schedule. I then continued my learning with a formal language school several times per week, followed with a masters course in Italian at Rutgers University, driving at least forty minutes a few times a week for one class.

Then, I lived in Florence for six weeks which entailed six-hour, one-on-one classes with a professor five days a week. Now, I take lessons via Skype three times a week with a professor in Florence. My language studies are ongoing, and I am driven to keep them up to better myself with the language. Thank you, persistence!

One of my favorite and heartfelt reminders about persistence is the persistent love I have for my husband.

Prior to our marriage, we went through some hurdles where I remember feeling so desperate that I became persistent at one thing: prayer. It felt as though that was the only thing that could save my heart. It was. Prayer was all I had left to resort to.

My husband and I are twenty years apart in age, and even though that doesn't faze us, it was difficult for others to accept especially for those close to us. We believed we were brought together for a reason and to serve a bigger purpose together, but they wondered how and why we were even dating. It felt like it was at least a two-year period where everyone around us doubted us. They doubted the true love we had for each other and the authenticity of our relationship.

So, I started to pray harder. I wasn't even a practicing Christian at the time, but I did believe in God. I prayed that He would open the eyes of our family and friends and allow them to see the true love Brian and I shared for one another. I also prayed that those difficult times would build our relationship and make us stronger, rather than tear us apart.

I remember persistently praying that same prayer every day for months. Why? Because I truly believed that God had placed that seed of love for Brian in my heart for a reason, a reason that I couldn't give up on. It was something we both had to fight for *together* at the beginning of our relationship, but it built such a solid foundation for us, and our love for each other grew stronger and stronger.

Our love was built on God's foundation, His decision to join our two hearts together. We could have given up and walked away from our relationship, but we didn't.

I prayed persistently and God delivered. Moreover, he helped build our love on solid ground.

There are so many opinions and judgments that we often allow to get in front of us, occupying our thoughts and emotions. As I said before, we must constantly retrain our brain to be only concerned with God's judgment. Are we living for Him and properly representing Him?

It's now been two years since my husband and I got married with all our family and friends surrounding us, and we honestly can't wait to see how God continues to use us to glorify Him. We are excited about the future and the unexpected, not only because we get to do it together, but because we know we are meant for more!

95

CIRCLE IT

Praying hard is two-dimensional: praying like it depends on God, and working like it depends on you.

—Mark Batterson

Dear God,

I am circling my prayer for my On Map On Mission event in January 2019. I want to sell out every seat of the Nourse Theater. I want to get a great leader from the Christian community to speak, and I want to get an awesome band to perform. I want to take all the knowledge and talents I have with event planning to help spread Your Word and Glorify Your name.

I know You're a God who delivers and You deliver abundantly. Nothing is too small for You, so that is why I am praying big.

Most importantly, I pray that You are in a front row seat at our event. That Your presence penetrates throughout the space and souls of everyone who attends. Nothing is more real, more peaceful and more beautiful than Your presence.

I have such a clear vision for this event and I keep replaying it over and over again in my mind. I am praying for Your help and Your miraculous blessings.

I love you,
Carrie

Through Mark Batterson's book, *The Circle Maker*, I have learned the power of prayer. I learned how praying *through* situations or hard times will get you *through* situations and hard times. I also learned how praying *big* makes me realize all the immeasurable things God can do. I can't be afraid to ask, for the Bible states, *"Ask and it will be given to you; seek and you will find; knock and the door will be opened to you"* (Matthew 7:7 NIV).

There is nothing God can't do and there is no prayer He doesn't answer. Sometimes the answer to our prayers isn't the answer we want to hear, but that means there is something better in store for us. Sometimes it takes the shock and reality of a situation we didn't expect to happen in order to appreciate the positive future outcomes. The key ingredient is staying faithful to God and praying *through* those times, trusting in His plan.

It's easy to play the victim card or complain to God about your situation, saying, "God this isn't fair. Why me?" In those moments, you are essentially saying, "God, you don't know what you're doing. You don't know what's fair, I do!" This is a slippery slope, when bad thoughts and the temptation to listen to the devil inside you takeover.

It's a test of your faith, trust, obedience, and commitment to God. He knows best because He knows all. We don't.

I also learned through this incredible book that persistent prayer is powerful. Outcomes to prayers don't always happen right away. Sometimes, it takes days, weeks, months, or years, but it's so awesome when you have been praying hard about something for a long time and then your prayer gets answered! Sometimes you have to go through some unforeseen hurdles to get there, and sometimes you may feel down and out, like it's never going to happen, but those are the times when you must keep your heart and mind focused on prayer and trusting in God the most.

We must also understand that sometimes a prayer isn't directly answered, and that requires the same continued prayer and trust.

Other times, when God answers things in a different way then you originally asked, you end up saying, "Thank God!" You never know what God's plan is so keep on praying!

Praying circles is praying hard. Praying circles draws spiritual circles around your visions and dreams. They require God's help and your dependence on God. They require leaning in on the Word. When times are tough, you pray on scripture to help you through.

If you are a person who is passionate, motivated, persistent, or driven about any aspect in life, then you can be persistent about prayer and draw infinite circles around your dreams. They will be answered.

I am drawing many circles around our upcoming On Map On Mission event. It feels like a "Hail Mary" in many ways. First of all, it's the first Christian event that I am ever hosting in our industry. Secondly, I have booked the Nourse Theater in San Francisco that has 1,600-plus seats, so I am fully committed to that. Thirdly, I am praying for a powerfully inspired speaker to agree to bring God's Word. Lastly, I am praying on the right band to headline the worship music. Sounds like a reach, right? Well, I'm praying circles around the Nourse Theater!

SURRENDER

In Italiano:

    Eccomi, sono qui

    Qui per Te

    Riempimi in profondità

    Ho fame di Te

    La mia vita offro a Te

    Mi arrendo

    Più di Te, più di Te

    Nel mio cuore, oh Signore

                  —Davide Di Lecce

In English:

    Here I am, I am here

    Here for You

    Fill me deeply

    I hunger for You

    I offer my life to You

    I surrender myself

    More of You, More of You

    In my heart, oh, Lord

H ow do we live a surrendered life to God? Simple. Matthew 16:24–25 explains it perfectly:

"Then Jesus told his disciples 'if anyone would come after me, let him deny himself and take up his cross and follow me. For whoever would save his life will lose it, but whoever loses his life for my sake will find it.'" (ESV)

God needs every piece of you. He can't just have 90 percent. In order for us to give Him our all, we must surrender to Him daily. I say daily because we are human and much of our natural instinct is to get distracted with other tasks and activities, or simply default to do the things *we want* first. Then we will get back to God.

Surrendering takes practice and requires much discipline, but as you give more and more of yourself to God, He is able to work through you more and more. It becomes a win-win situation! You are being fulfilled with your earthly purpose, and God is being glorified.

Personally, I say, "I surrender to you Jesus," every day. But how exactly do I put it into practice?

The previous scripture from the Gospel of Matthew says, *"Deny himself and take up his cross and follow me."* We must surrender *our self-will, our plans for our life,* and even *our pride* for *His* plan. He is the controller of our lives, not us. When things don't go our way, we have a difficult time handling that, but we must understand that it's one of two things: either the timing isn't right yet (according to God's clock) or He has a better plan in store for us.

We must learn to surrender our self-control. When pain, suffering or hard times arise in our lives, are we complaining and saying, "Why me?" or "God doesn't love me," or "God forgot about me," or are we saying, "Lord if this is your will for my life or the lives of others around me, then it will be done."

This daily surrender is a practice that requires dedicated commitment. It's not easy, but once that mentality and lifestyle are formed (one with Jesus) it is the truest path of living.

Much of surrendering to God is being obedient in our everyday lives and actions and, most importantly, through the attitude of our heart. We can be obedient and do everything we do on a daily basis—work, parenting, working out, cooking, anything really—for Him. All we need to do it focus that activity on doing it for God, and talk to Him while we do it! It's so simple!

It's as easy as the times when I was a young girl in school. I always wanted to work hard to get good grades, but I also wanted to impress the teacher. I wanted the teacher to be pleased with me too. God is the teacher for our lives. He created each of us for a specific purpose, so we should strive to please Him. We must surrender all we do for Him, and it's only through our acts of surrender that our purpose will shine.

There will always be hard times in life that test our obedience to God, but we must *"take up his cross."* It's not always easy to follow Jesus. At some point or another, you will probably be worried about family members or friends judging you. In fact, it may cost you some relationships to *"take up his cross"* and follow Jesus. However, you will be the one with a glorious relationship with our Lord, our God, and have everlasting life with Him in heaven.

So at the end of each day, check and see whose cross you are carrying. Are you carrying the heavy burdens of your own life: the worries, the judgments of others, the self-guilt and exhaustion of trying to please others? Or are you carrying the cross of Jesus where the *"burden is light"* (Matthew 11:30 NIV), but the path narrow.

This path is difficult to live by at times, but oh so rewarding! It's not the "default" wide-and-easy path that everyone takes, it's the path that those who want to be daughters and sons of God choose to take. This path leads back to their true home, back to their true Father. This path they must trust for one purpose, surrendering to God.

> *"Enter through the narrow gate. For wide is the gate and broad is the road that leads to destruction, and many enter through it. But small is the gate and narrow the road that leads to life, and only few find it"* *(Matthew 7:13–14 NIV).*

> *"For my yoke is easy and my burden is light"* *(Matthew 11:30 NIV).*

STAR STATUS

On this altar of dust and clay
A heart of stone now turned to praise
In Your presence my faith remains
I won't wander from this place…
Here I am, on this altar
Coming back in sweet surrender
Here I am, Yours forever
Be glorified, be glorified.

—Vive Worship

One night before bed, I was praying and asking God to speak to my heart. I asked Him to help me hear His words that will guide me to execute His perfect will, or for a specific word of guidance. Moments later, the phrase "Daniel 12" came into my mind. Nothing else.

I thought it was odd because I didn't really know the book of Daniel that well, especially chapter 12. I grabbed my Bible and began to read. I immediately noticed that this chapter is the last chapter in the book of Daniel and the title is "The End Times." There is much to absorb in this short chapter but what struck me the most was the verse, *"Those who lead many to righteousness, like the stars for ever and ever"* (Daniel 12:3 NIV).

I read it a few times, and even though it was the verse that stuck out to me, I wanted to lean in deeper with these specific words. I Googled the different versions of this verse and quickly came upon the beautiful Message Translation:

> *"And those who put others on the right path to life will glow like stars forever"* (Daniel 12:3 MSG).

After I read that, I thought to myself, "Now who doesn't want that?" I leaned back on my pillow and a huge smile came across my face as I remembered the special thing that happened just two days before.

It was a Sunday morning, so as usual, my husband and I went to our local church, Christ Fellowship in Royal Palm Beach Florida. It was a rainy day so I rushed inside and, from the corner of the lobby,

I heard someone calling my name. I immediately turned around to find one of my dear friends standing there. I was so surprised, but more so, overjoyed that she was there.

I only knew a little about her religious background. She grew up going to a Christian church but didn't have a very positive experience. To her, church felt more like a chore rather than seeing it as a way of growing a personal relationship with God. As a result, she stopped going to church several years ago.

So when I saw her standing there in the lobby of our church, you could understand the level of excitement I felt.

Soon after taking our seats, we learned that guest pastor, Charlotte Gambill, would be speaking. I not only was ecstatic to hear this news because I had been wanting to hear her speak for a while, but I knew deep inside that God had a special message in store for my friend.

The music started to play and the entire audience began to sing and worship together. I would glance out of the corner of my eye and see my friend singing, but her body language showed she was a little uncomfortable. I didn't say anything, I just let her be.

Song one and two finished, a third song, then another. I was thinking to myself that I hoped she was feeling a little more comfortable, and I took a quick glance to see her swaying, eyes closed, and taking it all in. I smiled, knowing once again that God always has a plan, revealed in His time and even in the smallest ways.

The sermon that Charlotte preached was amazing and as she began her closing prayer, she began to speak powerful words of truth. You could feel the energy of the Holy Spirit in the room and I could hear my friend start to cry.

I immediately grabbed her hand and she placed her other hand on top of mine. Having her second hand on top of mine was so important because a few seconds later, Pastor Charlotte asked something special to the audience, particularly for those who want to give their lives to Jesus and start living for Him. She asked for them to raise their hand. I was wondering what my friend was going to do at the exact moment I felt her hand disappear from the top of mine.

I didn't have to look. I knew. We were both crying, praying, and squeezing each other's hands. I know it was a moment that my friend will never forget, but it was also a moment that I will always cherish.

It was the first time I was used as a vessel of God's love to bring a friend directly to his altar to be saved. I literally could feel God using me to impact others in ways that I never would have thought of.

Fast forward to two days later, sitting in bed reading Daniel 12:3: *"And those who put others on the right path to life will glow like stars forever,"* made me feel good knowing God was happy. That verse felt like a congratulatory moment from God and a greater form of motivation to do it again!

My mind began to meditate even more on this verse and it became clear to me that these words were exactly what I needed to hear for another reason.

For months prior to this event, I had been praying for direction about my writings and journaling to see if they were actually something I should publish to the world. I wasn't sure because I didn't know if my words would be inspiring or relatable to others, or if they were simply journal entries for me to keep private. So I was struggling with clarity, but here was my answer. Crystal clear.

A direct message from God to "put others on the right path to life" through my book. It was as if God was saying, "You got this! Go do it!" And I knew then that I had to put it all together and put it out there. I had to put myself aside, because it's not about me. It's about Him.

Even if only *one* person reads this book, and grows closer to the Lord, like my one friend that came to church with me, it would be worth it to me. It would be worth all the work of writing every single word in this book.

FEAR:
THE KILLER OF TRUTH

Fear, you don't own me
There ain't no room in this story
And I ain't got time for you

—Francesca Battistelli

We all have fears. Fears of heights, fears of being alone, fears of regret, fears of missing out (a.k.a. FOMO), fears of judgment, fears of being unpopular, fears of the unknown, fears of self-image… The list goes on and on.

Fear is the killer of greatness. Fear is what holds you back and gets in the way of you being your best you. As you journey closer in your relationship with God, sometimes fear creeps in. We start to fear trusting Him with our whole heart, and we allow outside noises and distractions to get into our thoughts. These are the times that are truly testing our faith and the attitudes of our hearts.

Are you living a fear-based life or are you living a free and purposeful life for God? I have learned over time that during difficult situations or fearful moments, I must immediately focus my eyes on Jesus. If I allow people or situations to pull me away from the main focus of my life, I know that once I refocus back on Him, I will be able to see the situation differently. In a *Christlike* way.

Instead of reacting in my default, "human" way, I am able to step back, see the lesson being taught, see the positive in the circumstance, and refer to God's Word to bring me back to a place of truth.

When I initially decided that I was going to publish this book, I felt a little fear creep up inside. It wasn't fear of whether my writings would be perfect, or even liked by everyone. It was more a fear of what would people around me (i.e. family, friends, neighbors, etc.) think of me.

As this trickle of fear came to mind, I quickly realized that I can't live for me, because it's not about me. It's about Him. I refocused my thoughts and asked myself, "Am I here on earth to try to please people's ever-changing opinions and seek approval through their judgments? Or am I here on earth to fulfill a greater mission that glorifies God and seeks His approval?" I had to remind myself not to let fear (a.k.a the devil) separate me from my relationship with God. I had to replay the *Hillsong United* lyrics in my mind, "Let the devil know, not today!"

At the end of the day, when our souls pass to the gates of heaven, we will be held accountable and judged by the highest Judge there is, for it is written:

> *"Why do you judge your brother or sister? Or why do you treat them with contempt? For we will all stand before God's judgment seat...so then, each of us will give an account of ourselves to God"* (Romans 14:10–12 NIV).

So it was made perfectly clear to me, that I must cast my fears aside and wake to the fact that this feeling was a perfect opportunity to grow my faith even stronger. To trust Jesus even more and trust His Word, because His Word is truth.

Truth overcomes fear and anxiety. His Truth is the same yesterday, today, and tomorrow. God's Word is the Truth. People's opinions, judgments, and fears will try to change the truth. They say things like, "The truths in the Bible happened so long ago, and human society and culture has changed so much since then, that those truths don't apply anymore!" That statement or train of thought couldn't be further from the truth!

Truth doesn't change, it stays the same. So if the Word of the Bible is God's truth, and Jesus was the living flesh of God's Word, then Jesus is *truth*!

"I am the way and the truth and the life"
(John 14:6 NIV).

When fear tries to attack and get in the way of our relationship with Jesus, we must remind ourselves to speak and think words of truth.

It's thrilling and exciting for me to be writing these words without one ounce of fear in my body. My purpose is to spread His good news, please only Him, and speak the truth.

> *"One night the Lord spoke to Paul in a vision: 'Do not be afraid; keep on speaking, do not be silent. For I am with you, and no one is going to attack and harm you'" (Acts 18:9–10 NIV).*

PRACTICE THINKING

Do not conform to the pattern of this world, but
be transformed by the renewing of your mind.

—Romans 12:2

I t is a daily choice to be a disciple of Christ. To become more *Christlike* in all your thoughts, words, and actions. To achieve this goal, it all starts with your thoughts. It reminds me of the saying, "You are what you think." Thoughts are so powerful. They create our imagination, future visions, goals, beliefs, and form our actions.

Thoughts are also quite difficult to control. It takes much discipline, practice, and patience to keep your mind in order. That's why becoming *Christlike* is not something that happens overnight. Rather, one must practice renewing the mind on a daily basis.

I love the entire book of Romans, but my favorite verses are nine through twenty-one of chapter twelve. These lines tell us exactly how to live and think every day. If everyone lived by these simple thirteen lines, the world would be a much more peaceful place. For many though, this kind of thinking is difficult and would require a drastic shift in their character. But guess what, the Apostle Paul tells us through these verses in his letter to the Romans to *"not conform to the pattern of the world."* In other words, don't practice evil to one another, don't look down upon those who are less fortunate than you, don't be proud or conceited, don't take revenge upon others—don't fall into the bad habit traps of this world.

We know better and we were made for better, for it is written that, He *"set his seal of ownership on us, and put His Spirit in our hearts as a deposit, guaranteeing what is to come"* (2 Corinthians 1:22 NIV).

I love this verse because it's not only telling us how we are His, and how we have a piece of Him in us (the Holy Spirit), but at any time we can channel the Holy Spirit and connect with God. He is never too far away. He is in us.

> *"For we know that when this earthly tent we*
> *live in is taken down (that is, when we die and leave*
> *this earthly body), we will have a house in Heaven,*
> *an eternal body made for us by God himself and not*
> *by human hands"* (2 Corinthians 5:1 NLT).

Our Spirit is His. He created us to connect with Him, live in His honor on this temporary earth by choosing to live in ways like His Son, Jesus. All this so that we can go home to Him in our eternal house that will be waiting for us.

This all seems like one giant and intimidating thought. Thinking about death and Heaven is often scary for many, but think of it like this: that's our true home. We were destined for heaven, it's just that it feels so unknown to most of us. I can promise you that the more you renew your thoughts to becoming more *Christlike* on a daily basis, the more you will start thinking about that future day you get to meet Jesus face to face. That thought is far from daunting, it's comforting.

> Surrounded by Your glory
> What will my heart feel?
> Will I dance for you, Jesus,
> Or in awe of You be still?
> Will I stand in your presence
> Or to my knees will I fall?

Will I sing hallelujah?
Will I be able to speak at all?
I can only imagine
I can only imagine

—MercyMe

REFLECTION

On the mountains I will bow my life to the One
who set me there
In the valley I will lift my eyes to the One who
sees me there
When I'm standing on the mountain I didn't get
there on my own
When I'm walking through the valley I know I
am not alone
You're God of the hills and valleys

—Tauren Wells

This song played on repeat in my mind as I *walked through a valley* in my life. These lines reminding me that God is with me and that I'm never alone have never felt more true than they did for me at a very specific moment of my recent past. It's easy to praise God when things are great and easy in life, or when you're standing on that "mountain top." The test is how you praise and communicate with God during the hard times (a.k.a the valleys).

I take these difficult times as a reminder to reset my mind every day on what is really most important in life, Jesus. Who really knows me better then I know myself? Jesus. Who really knows every moment of my past and every step I will take in the future? Jesus. Who has a greater plan for my life, even when things don't go the way I plan? Jesus. This life is not my own. I am here *because* of Jesus and I am here *for* Jesus.

As a human, my brain defaults to thinking that this life is for me. I can do what I want, when I want, and everything should go my way. That is a false reality. If you continue to live that way and with those thoughts, you will live a life without purpose and in the end, feel empty inside.

My life's purpose is serving Jesus. Serving Jesus is not always an easy road, but I must continually remind myself that the path He wants me to walk down serves a greater purpose, and is bigger than anything I can try to imagine.

I love journaling about the times God has directly answered my prayers. I know he is always answering our prayers whether we like the answers or not. It's awesome though when I pray and He answers right away, as if He is talking with me on the phone or right there with me.

Some prayers take years to be answered and others moments. These moments are great reminders to me that God is always present even when he seems physically far away. Even when you are walking through the dark valleys (shadows of death), He sees you, and He will step in and save you at exactly the right moment that you need saving. That is our God!

It's amazing for me to think about how there are billions of people on this planet and every single one of us are different. No two people are the same. A miracle. We're not just unique in appearance; every single one of us is here for a unique purpose. Like me, some of us have read books, studied, researched, and meditated on the concept of what life's purpose is, and how it can be discovered. The truth is that there is only one way to discover your life's purpose. One. You must fix your eyes on Jesus. When you put Jesus first in everything you do, your life will flow with purpose and you will be overflowing with His glory.

Let me break it down a little more. When you wake up every day thanking God for another day on this planet, when you give God your problems and concerns during hard times, when you praise Him for the great things in your life, when you talk to Him in your thoughts or out loud throughout the day, when you read His Word daily, when you serve others with love, compassion, and kindness as if they are your brothers and sisters, when you become an active member in God's church, when you keep your eyes fixed on Jesus and put Jesus first, your daily purpose and lifelong mission will be unveiled before you.

Jesus created you, and as Pastor Rick Warren says, "He has the owner's manual to your life." So why would you depend on anyone else for guidance?

This is all very overwhelming and challenging to hear and think about because it goes against many aspects of human society and cultural rules that we have created for ourselves.

In general, humans naturally want to judge others, judge ourselves, put ourselves first, look down on the poor, envy the wealthy, and we find it easier to receive rather than give. Putting Jesus first requires you to transform your thoughts and actions while still remaining true to the personal character traits that God created in each of us. He wants us to use our strengths to glorify Him, help others, and spread His love and great works.

This is both a challenge *and* the best choice you will ever make. It's this positive decision that makes you shine as a person and the energy you emulate will be addictive! Others will notice it and want it! God's love is contagious!

I could write about God all day. Just writing these words is getting me excited for the unexpected, for what's to come next! Why? Because I know it will be good! I trust God with all my heart and I know that He will never steer one of His children in a bad direction, just as parents wouldn't do to their children. God is our true Father and I know He loves me.

NEW WINE

They have no more wine

—John 2:3

Many people have heard the phrase "Give it to God," especially when someone is going through a hard time or is worried about someone or something. This phrase is easy to say but much more difficult to put into practice. When you give your worries (the things that are out of your control) to God, you literally feel lighter. You feel at peace. You have done all that you can do, now give it to God. Let Him tell you what to do next. Learn to smile and welcome the unexpected!

I'm reminded of the story of Jesus turning water into wine. Many people, when they reference or talk about this story, focus on the actual miracle of Jesus turning the water into wine, and while I love that part of the story too, I like to recall the behind-the-scenes part more.

Anne Graham Lotz, author of the incredible book, *Just Give Me Jesus,* painted this scene so perfectly and inspired me to write down my reflections of the story.

She opens the scene with Jesus attending a wedding in Galilee, and one of the guests in attendance was his mother Mary. The author explains how during this time, it was very important that guests had fun throughout the entire celebration which included an abundance of wine and food. People ate and drank to their fullest. One other important factor was that it was unheard of for the wine to run out at a party like this. There was *always* backup, so when the "A Grade" wine ran out, there was always an inventory of "B Grade" wine to fill the guests' cups. If, by chance, *all* the wine ran out, it would be like switching the lights on at a party, with everyone gasping and gossiping behind the bride's and groom's back. It would be utterly humiliating.

So, when Mary heard that the wine was gone (probably from to one of the servants), she went right to Jesus. What she said to Jesus is the best part of the story to me. She didn't go to him and tell him what *she needed* or *wanted* him to do and she didn't tell him to talk to a certain person. She just said, "They have no more wine." That's it. She stated the problem.

Since she was his mother and knew him very well, she knew that he would know how to fix the problem and, more importantly, would handle it exactly the right way and at exactly the right time. She trusted him with the problem one hundred percent.

As a result, he went to the servants and instructed them on what to do, and made the water turn into wine. And He didn't just turn the water into any old kind of wine, but rather the finest wine of the day.

Anne Lotz's interpretation of the story resonated so deeply with me because it's something I must practice every day. If a situation is out of my hands, I try not to waste time worrying about it. I give it to God. Tell Jesus the exact problem. When the time is right, He will deliver! He will deliver the best for you, and the best is yet to come!

AWE–SOME

You are my strength and comfort
You are my steady hand
You are my firm foundation
The rock on which I stand
Your ways are always higher
Your plans are always good
There's not a place where I'll go
You've not already stood

—Lauren Daigle

As much as I travel, I sometimes freak myself out with the "what ifs" in life. *What if* something happens to me and there is no hospital around? *What if* something happens to my husband during our travels? *What if* I am in a foreign country and get lost and can't understand the language? *What if* my car breaks down and the country I'm in doesn't have AAA? *What if* my plane crashes? All of these "what ifs."

Through these frantic or panicked moments of thinking, I have learned to turn the question around. *What if* God is with me all the time? *What if* God sees my every move and only has a good plan for me? *What if* nothing can stop God's plan? *What if* every moment serves a purpose and will bring good out of the situation?

When I retrain my brain, I turn the stress off inside of me and bask in the peace and calmness of His Spirit.

It's amazing how bringing my heart, soul, and mind back to Jesus and statements of truth quickly readjusts my thoughts to focus on my positive purpose, rather than the possible daunting and hypothetical future situations which I can't control.

I had such a wonderful and peaceful day recently while enjoying one of my favorite cities in God's world, Montalcino, Italy, but the day started off a little differently.

As I woke up, I immediately realized that I was not feeling a hundred percent. My throat was bothering me and I developed a bit of a hacking cough. I didn't want to, but I told my husband that it would probably be best for him to go to Florence with our friends for the day without me. I felt the need to catch up on some sleep and take it easy. Of course, he understood, so he honored my request and headed off to Florence.

After sleeping until noon (which I hadn't done in forever), I decided it was time to get up and get something to eat. I took my cough syrup (after a five-minute coughing fit) and got ready to go down to the hotel restaurant.

I was definitely feeling a little down because it was such a glorious day outside, but every time I took a deep breath in, I coughed several times. I was continually praying for God to heal my sickness and make me feel better.

Upon entering the lobby, I noticed that no tables were set and the restaurant doors were closed. I asked the hotel staff if they were serving lunch and they explained that the dining room was for breakfast and dinner only. I then asked where the closest restaurant was and they said that it would be best to go into town. Without a car or shuttle (which the hotel didn't provide) it would be a thirty-minute walk along steep terrain into town (FYI, the city of Montalcino is located on the top of a mountain, 564 meters above sea level).

Let's just say a little panic, combined with hangry syndrome (when the feelings of hunger and anger mix into a lovely frustrating feeling), started to set in. I felt alone and a little nervous about my journey through the windy, curvy, steep mountain roads. I already wasn't feeling very good, and I started to let the devil get the best of me with negative and distracting thoughts.

What if something happens to me and Brian will have no clue? What if I pass out or have a seizure while I'm hiking alone on the side of the road? Suddenly, the vast countryside of Tuscany started to close in on me and I began to feel scared. Quickly snapping my brain out of its default ways of thinking, I told myself that Jesus is with me and I reminded myself of the scripture verse, *"Do not be afraid... He will never leave you nor forsake you"* (Deuteronomy 31:6 NIV).

I told myself, "He is walking by my side right now on this hillside road." Then I started to talk out loud to Him. I'm sure if anyone walked by, they would think I was crazy, but it felt relaxing and put my mind at ease, talking to Him while I walked. He helped me every step on the steep hike, and I could feel my climb become His climb too.

As I was talking to Him, I started thanking Him for everything He has given me in life. I expressed my fears to Him and I told Him that I will live for Him every day. Then, after a moment, I thought about that last sentence, *I will live for Him*, and said to myself that, "If I am living for Him every day of my life, what is there to be afraid of? He is an awesome God and only wants to do awesome things through me! Living a life like that doesn't sound scary!"

At that point on my hike to lunch, the winding road made a sharp turn. As I lifted my head to see what was ahead, I saw the Glory of Jesus there before me. I stopped and had to catch my breath, not because of the huge climb I just made, but because of the most unbelievable view in front of me. ✳

I was in awe of the panoramic vista that stretched out before my eyes. The infinite rolling hills of Tuscany—as far as my eyes could see—and out in front of me was the beautiful walled city of Montalcino, perched on top a mountain directly parallel to where I had stopped. It was absolutely silent where I was standing except for the birds chirping in the distance. I stood there in complete awe and said "Wow!" out loud. I thought to myself, "This is You, Jesus. This is Your vastness, Your abundance, Your glory, and Your overwhelming beauty. "

It was a moment to live for, a moment when God was quite literally speaking to me. He was telling me that He was with me. Furthermore, He was everywhere I looked. If you take the time to *look* each day, you will find Him too, no matter where you are in the world.

From that moment, I decided that this day was going to be my "date day" with Jesus. We were going to have lunch together, walk the town together, and hike back to the hotel together. He would be my friend to talk to (both internally and out loud), and he would protect and watch over me.

The rest of the day was fun, calm, relaxing, and peaceful. Thinking and talking to Jesus all day made me even more aware of His presence all around me, and appreciate each moment of being alive. All of a sudden, all of those "what if" thoughts felt so far away... as if they were in the distant hills of Tuscany, and I thought to myself, "Why shouldn't every day be a 'date day' with Jesus?"

* Couldn't help but think what she would have missed if she had her head buried in her iphone or some other hand held device. What is it in life that we miss because we are so preoccupied with the many distractions of today?! Keep our eyes on JESus and be alert to what spectacular "view" He wants to show you and me.

IL GIRASOLE

Italian translation for sunflower:

Gira: turn, twist, or rotate.

Sole: sun.

E very day they wake from their slumber at the exact moment they feel Your heat rising onto the earth.

Their petals and large center discs lift upward as Your rays beam down from the sky.

Their energy source is You.

Their path during the days is following You.

They slowly turn their faces throughout the day in the direction that You move.

Their life is You.

Without You they can't function.

Without You they can't survive.

Without You their name would be meaningless.

Who are we to not observe these creations of Yours, and with the seed of righteousness sewn in our hearts, choose the everlasting path of Light like the sunflower.

John 8:12

" ... Jesus said "I am the light of the world. Whoever follows me will never walk in darkness, but will have the light of life!""

John 12:46

Jesus said " I have come into the world as a light, so that no one who believes in me should stay in darkness".

MARS, NOT THE PLANET

Though the seasons change
Your love remains

—United Persuit

I recently visited the city of Athens in Greece and was blown away by one spot in particular.

It's not the spot that most people think of which dates back to the fifth century BC and sits on a glorious hill overlooking the five million inhabitants of Athens; the Parthenon (i.e. the Acropolis).

It's not one of the other famous tourist attractions of the city—the oldest Olympic stadium that dates back to the sixth century BC, which holds about fifty-thousand spectators and is constructed entirely of marble; the Panathenaic Stadium.

The spot I am referring to is a prominent rock located just outside the entrance to the Acropolis. Yes, you read correctly, a rock. If you happened to be walking on the trail that leads to the Acropolis, you would probably walk right by it if it wasn't for all the tourists standing on top snapping pictures and selfies. Why did this one boulder in particular leave a mark on my heart? This was the exact spot Paul stood and shared one of his most powerful messages during his time in the city, and one which we read about today in the New Testament.

This place I am describing is called Mars Hill—coined by the Romans of the time—but to many, it was known as Areopagus (translated from Ancient Greek meaning "big piece of rock").

As I stood on top of this "big piece of rock" that has a breathtaking panoramic view of the city of Athens, and is situated ever so slightly under the Acropolis, I closed my eyes and tried to imagine the day Paul stood there, thousands of years ago. How cool would it have been to not only be sitting there listening to him speak, but I was also imagining the Acropolis in its true beauty (not the ruins we see today). I imagined the hustling of all the people in the ancient local town marketplace, known as the Agora, which is mostly ruins today except for one main building that is well preserved.

The view from this rock was outstanding and the Resurrection message preached was unforgettable. I couldn't wait to get back to my hotel room and open up my bible to read further details about this memorable time in history on Mars Hill.

As I was reading Acts 17:16–32, the story came to life for me in a very special way. It explains that during the time that Paul was in Athens, he was very upset to see that so many people in the city were worshiping false gods.

> *"So he argued in the synagogue with the Jews and the devout persons, and also in the marketplace every day with those who happened to be there"* (Acts 17:17 NRSV).

I immediately thought of the ancient marketplace ruins of the Agora that I saw while overlooking the city. My mind was journeying back in time thinking about all the old artifacts that we saw on display at the marketplace. I was envisioning the local people cooking with their beautifully handmade clay pots and pans. I imagined them pouring the wine and olive oil out from their detailed painted vases and urns, and I couldn't forget the tiny pieces of gold bracelets and rings that were found in the excavation grounds. I'm reminded how times have changed so much since then, yet in ways, have remained the same.

I smiled thinking how we use many of the same style cookware today (just made out of different materials), how we wear the same style jewelry, and how we hold in our hearts the same words that were spoken about Jesus. The powerful words that Paul shared back then about Jesus' resurrection are just as powerful today.

Through Paul's words, he was able to bring insight and knowledge to many people, and as a result, he influenced them to believe in the Good News about Jesus. He was passionate about bringing awareness to the people that worshiping false gods is ignorant and there is only one true God:

> *"The God who made the world and everything in it is the Lord of heaven and earth and does not live in temples built by human hands"* (Acts 17:24 NIV).

He then proceeds to explain:

> *"For in him we live and move and have our being"* (Acts 17:28 NIV).

People became intrigued and inspired by Paul and wanted to hear more. He continued to talk and spread the news about Jesus until he finally decided that it was time to leave Athens and head toward the city of Corinth.

I was even more intrigued by this entire chapter of the bible after having visited the actual site. That rock, boulder, or hill (however you want to refer to it), became such a monumental place in Christian history. God was moving mountains (or rocks) through Paul back then, and continues to do so through us today!

"Because of the littleness of your faith; for truly I say to you, if you have faith the size of a mustard seed, you will say to this mountain, 'Move from here to there,' and it will move; and nothing will be impossible to you" (Matthew 17:20 NASB).

ON MAP ON MISSION

Don't bother like you've gotta do it all
Just let Jesus use you where you are
One day at a time

—Josh Wilson

Wherever you are right now, you are being called by God to serve a great mission.

Serving others doesn't always mean you have to be on a mission trip in Africa, Guatemala, or another part of the world helping the poor. That is amazing if you are doing that right now, but God wants to use you *wherever* you are on the map. Whether that point on the map is at work in an office setting, or a doctor or nurse in a hospital, or a trainer at a gym, or a teacher at a school, or a stay-at-home mom or dad—wherever you are, you are being called to serve His purpose.

Each one of us has unique talents, characteristics, strengths, and weaknesses, and God wants to use all those attributes that he created in you to help others and in turn, have others help you.

There is no other *you* in this world. You are the only *you* in this moment right now, exactly where you are, and that's why the people you come in contact with each day are different than who I come in contact with. Your service is different than mine, but we both share the same mission: to serve God.

In the Bible, Jesus says that the greatest commandment in the law is, *"Love the Lord your God with all your heart and with all your soul and with all your mind. This is the first and greatest commandment. And the second is like it: Love your neighbor as yourself"* (Matthew 22:37-39 NIV).

With everyone you meet and come in touch with, you have the ability to leave a lifelong impression. You have the ability to serve God by spreading the news about Jesus and all he has done for us.

This doesn't necessarily mean that you have to start pouring out the gospel to every person that you meet. Instead, we can spread

Jesus' word on a smaller scale. How are you reflecting a *Christlike* character to others? Are you showing compassion, kindness, gentleness, patience, humbleness, generosity, gladness, and love?

Even though none of us are perfectly wired in all these ways, as we are not perfect beings, we do have some of these attributes and it's important to always move toward bettering ourselves in as many of these ways as possible.

When you begin to treat others with these sincere acts of love, then you will have an influence on them. It's in these ways that you are also personally growing in a spiritual way, and strengthening your personal relationship with God.

God loves seeing us help and love each other. That is what he created us to do. We are all uniquely different in order to serve a uniquely different purpose.

Whether you are literally on a mission trip right now, or at your office desk, you are part of a global mission.

Don't ever think that you are not important, or that you don't have a purpose. Those thoughts are allowing the devil to distract you from God's good plan for your life.

I encourage you to take a look around, see who God has placed in your life (either for a lifetime or a moment), and ask God how you can help serve that person.

Maybe it's showing compassion to a friend who is going through a difficult time. Maybe it's showing patience toward someone who always manages to get on your nerves. Maybe it's surprising someone with kind and loving words in a card or email. Maybe its volunteering your time to help at a local charity. These are all ways of serving right now, exactly where you are.

One other beautiful thing to note is that it is *never* too late to start serving! Remember, the way you treat people will always be remembered. The relationships you build on earth are the legacy you leave, not the material and temporary things that you accumulate.

Like the greatest commandment says, put your time and energy into serving God and each other. *That* is what your *mission* on this *map* is all about.

> *"The Fruit of the Spirit is love, joy, peace, forbearance, kindness, goodness, faithfulness, gentleness and self-control"* *(Galatians 5:22–23 NIV).*

> *"So we fix our eyes not on what is seen, but on what is unseen, since what is seen is temporary, but what is unseen is eternal"* *(2 Corinthians 4:18 NIV).*

TRUE JEWELS

We're more beautiful when we come togeth-
er-let's stand united!

—Mandisa

I have always loved the beauty of jewelry. I love learning about all the different types of stones, the different cuts, shapes, colors, and the infinite designs that can be created with some of earth's finest gemstones.

I love the different shades of red that rubies can be, and the brilliant blue of a lapis stone, the rainbow sparkle of a diamond, or the perfect shine of the finest gold. They are all beautiful individually, but when put together as a designed piece, they often create an outstanding work of art that leaves you in awe.

Whether the piece you are in awe of is on your wrist, finger, neck, or in the window of a jewelry store, it catches your eye and you have to stop and stare.

The other reason why I love jewelry is the stories behind each piece. Whether you are wearing something you bought for yourself on a specific occasion, or it was given to you as a gift, or you inherited it as a family heirloom, each piece tells a story, a unique story that no one else can share.

My grandmother, who lived to be ninety-six, recently died. We shared a love for many things including jewelry. I loved going over to her house and listening to all the stories behind each of her beautiful pieces. These times that we shared together were special ones that I will cherish forever, because it was a way for her and I to journey back in time together and share some of her fondest memories. One story would always lead to another, and another, and I would end up learning so much about the people in her life, the places she traveled to and most importantly, her.

Since her passing, I was gifted with a beautiful ring of hers, but it's not the ring that is important to me, it's the story behind it. Of course, I was deeply saddened when my grandmother died, but I'm so grateful to have known her for thirty-five years of my life. God placed her in my life for me to grow as a person. I smile every day, knowing her influence is with me, because she has shaped me in so many ways. I would not be me without her influence.

While many of us grow to appreciate and accumulate jewelry, shoes, and clothes over the years, I have learned to appreciate the *true jewels* in life. The jewels that can't be found in mines, volcanoes, the depths of the ocean, or adorned on the body of a human. The kind of jewels that aren't tangible or visible.

The jewels I am referring to are the stunning, glimmering, and eternal jewels of hope, salvation, wisdom, understanding, and love.

Jewels like these are the most precious gems. They create the true color, clarity, and sparkle in one's life. To adorn yourself with true wisdom and understanding is like a diamond glistening in the sun light. You are unscratchable, but have a clear and transparent softness that others gravitate toward.

In order to grasp what true wisdom and understanding are in life, one only need look to The Bible. The Bible is God's Word. To have pure understanding in life is leaning into God.

"And he said to the human race, The fear of the Lord—that is wisdom, and to shun evil is understanding" (Job 28:28 NIV).

Through His Word, you will be shaped into the unique jewel that you were designed to be, and can be used with other unique gemstones to create one, united, remarkable piece of jewelry. Together, we become a powerful force of radiant light. We become a master-piece of art that glorifies our creator and designer.

It's important to learn about the unique jewels that lie inside of us, whether it's the talents and passions we were born with, or the lessons and character traits we've learned through our connections with others around us.

We must take the time to discover how we can use our beautiful gems to serve God and how we can collectively, through the church, help spread the love and news of the most precious jewel, Jesus.

FIGHT WITH FAITH

I've seen You move, You move the mountains
And I believe, I'll see You do it again
You made a way, where there was no way
And I believe, I'll see You do it again

—Elevation Worship

E very time I visit with my in-laws, I always leave saying the same thing to myself, "I need to do this more often." They live in the countryside of New Jersey, where it's easy to slip into the peace and serenity that surrounds you. I reboot and recharge myself when I visit with them, specifically on a spiritual level.

Both of my parents-in-law are devoted Christ followers, and are beautiful examples of how we can love the Lord with all of our hearts.

My mother-in-law, Fran Pasch, and I love to take a few hours when we are together and "spend time with the Lord" (i.e., dive into the Bible together). She has developed a deeper relationship with the Lord over the past thirty years and hosts a writers group in her local community. She also writes phenomenal poetry. My favorite is her book entitled *Double Vision: Seeing God In Everyday Life Through Devotions and Poetry.* Let's just say that I always leave their house with a deeper understanding of the Lord, which teaches me how to live a better life in closer fellowship with Him.

My recent trip to their house left my head spinning with ideas to journal about, but the one that stuck with me the most was the question I proposed to Fran after we read Hebrews 11 together.

If you have never read (or don't remember clearly) this chapter in the Bible, I will quickly sum it up for you. The dominant theme that is addressed is the true meaning of faith and what it really means to *live by faith.*

Opening up this chapter, we find a strong definition of the word faith: "*Faith is confidence in what we hope for and assurance about what we do not see*" (Hebrews 11:1 NIV).

A few verses later it goes onto say, "*Without faith it is impossible to please God*" (Hebrews 11:6 NIV).

Following these two bold statements, the chapter lists essential people in the Bible, many of whom you have probably heard of before, including Moses, Noah, Abraham, David, and others that lived faith-based lives.

Their number-one priority in life was their faith in God. Many of them had so much faith in God that, even though they were never able to see their full purpose lie before them, they continued to believe and live life by faith.

For example, Moses led the Israelites through the Red Sea and performed many other miracles in order to help lead them to the Promised Land, but he never actually ended up seeing the Promised Land himself. Rather, he helped pave the way for Joshua to lead the Israelites into the Promised land. Moses kept the faith and believed he was part of God's bigger purpose.

Sometimes the idea of *keeping the faith* can be something that's a lot easier said than done. For example, when you decide to accept God into your life and become a follower of Jesus, it may seem like life around you is still in turmoil and nothing has changed for the positive like you had expected. The only new addition may be that people are now starting to judge your decision to follow Jesus in a negative way? Is keeping the faith so easy then? After making this decision, you may expect everything to be immediately better in life, but sometimes faith requires you to fight for it. It requires you to fight the battle.

Noah is a great example of someone who had to fight with faith. God called him to build an ark in the middle of the desert. Not only had Noah never seen an ocean or a boat before, there had never even been rain on the planet prior to this time. But there Noah was, in the middle of the desert, keeping the faith and building a boat.

People thought Noah was nuts, but Noah didn't care. Through his faithfulness and obedience to God, he built the boat in precisely the way God ordered and saved his family from a flood that killed all other humans living on the earth at that time.

Noah had to fight with faith against the people who surrounded him and mocked him on a daily basis. He had to reassure himself regularly that his faith was built on a strong foundation with God, and that he was doing the right thing.

I love reading scripture stories like these because they feel so powerful and miraculous, but at the same time, they can also feel a little distant and hard to relate to.

I posed this question to Fran, "How do you effectively communicate God's goodness to others and encourage them to *fight with faith* when bad things happen?"

We agreed that this is definitely a hard situation, whether you are the person going through a difficult time in life or the one trying to comfort someone going through a hard time in life. What do you say? How do you respond?

What do you say to your friend whose marriage seemed to have fallen apart overnight? What do you say to your friend who was just diagnosed with cancer? What do you say to a friend who just lost a loved one in their life?

I was asking her because I wanted answers to all these questions. I wanted to know how I can be a light to others and encourage them to stay faithful to God, how I can help them fight with faith during hard times. I wanted her to understand that I want to be compassionate and sympathetic.

Let's just say that this was the start to a four-hour conversation, and since I had just finished reading the book of Job, he immediately came to my mind with this topic.

I think Job is one of the most relatable people in the Bible. Job was a man of God who trusted the Lord with all his heart, and also lived a very prosperous life during his time...until one day. One day, he was left with nothing; everything had been taken from him. Everything.

He lost his house in one day. He lost all his children in one day. He lost all his livestock in one day. He went from rich to poor in one day. He went from healthy to ill in one day. He went from happiness and joy to misery and depression in one day. He went from feeling on top of the world to feeling the world got ripped out from under him. All in one day.

Have you ever felt that way? Like your world just got turned upside down in one day?

I know I have felt that way, and I know that I could relate to how Job felt.

Job had a strong foundation with God which eventually saved him, but during the heat of it all he felt angry, upset, and frustrated with God. He felt that God was against him and didn't love or care for him anymore (which is never the case), but he began to ask *why* and in turn, doubt God.

He began to claim things weren't fair and in turn, imply that he knew better then God. He wanted to know *why?* Why him? He was searching for answers.

Through the book of Job and spending time with the Lord and Fran, I learned that it's not about having *all* the answers, because we will never have all the answers. We can't even begin to comprehend everything in this world that already exists, let alone future events that haven't happened yet. We weren't made to know all the answers. Only God knows and has *all* the answers.

When God finally responded to Job, he began to challenge him on his knowledge of *all* things:

> *"Then the Lord spoke to Job... 'where were you when I laid the earth's foundation...? Have you seen the gates of the deepest darkness...? Have you comprehended the vast expanses of the earth? Tell me, if you know all this."*

He continued to say:

> *"Do you send the lightning bolts on their way? Do they report to you, 'Here we are'? Who has the wisdom to count the clouds? Do you watch when the doe bears her fawn? Do you count the months till they bear?"* (Job 38-39 NIV).

After reading that, it became quite evident to me that we can't even begin to *try* to understand and have *all* the answers in life. So spinning our heads and searching for them is pointless.

As our discussion progressed, the question for me was no longer *why*, but rather, *where*.

Where is my focus when my world seems upside down like it did for Job, and suffering starts to overtake me? *Where* is my trust, like it was for Noah and Moses, that our God is a God of promises and miracles and has made me part of a bigger and greater plan? One that I may not actually be able to see in that moment of pain. *Where is my hope* like all the other faithful leaders mentioned in Hebrews 11 had?

Are your eyes fixed on all the unknown answers in life, or are they fixed on Jesus? The one and only answer.

> I know the sorrow, and I know the hurt
> Would all go away if You'd just say the word
> But even if You don't
> My hope is You alone
>
> —MercyMe

DAILY DEVOTIONAL

BE STILL

I created this next piece with the hope that you will read it, meditate on it, and remind yourself of it on a daily basis. The devotional is based on one of my favorite Bible verses that I have referenced through-out this book, and although its a short and simple verse, it is so packed with an impactful message.

I pray that you keep the following devotional close to your heart and bring it to mind on a daily basis—freshening your soul and most importantly, your perspective on life.

When troubles, problems, your darkest moments hit, remember to… *Be still.*

Literally, stop.

Be still in that moment, and remind yourself that *He. Is. God.*

> *"Be still and know that I am God"*
> (Psalm 46:10 NIV)

This verse is a promise that…

Our God is a powerful God.

Our God is a God of the Impossible. There is nothing He can't do. He defeated death!

Our God is an Ever Present God. He is a God of the past, the present and the future. He is the only one that knows you better then you know yourself. He can read your heart and knows the thoughts in your mind before they are even spoken.

Our God is a God of Love and Compassion. He wants to use our imperfections and hard times to channel His Grace through us. Allowing us to see how God can work through us even when we feel that we are at our lowest point. He uses these qualities and times in our life as opportunities of growth for us and ways to bless others around us.

Our God is a Forgiving God. There is no sin too great that can separate you from His love.

Our God is a Generous God. When we put Him first in our heart and our life, He blesses us abundantly.

Our God is our True Father. He teaches us, guides us, loves us and helps us to be better people by building lasting relationships with one another, building His Kingdom and leaving a lasting legacy while we are here on this earth—until we finally meet Him in our real home in heaven.

Our God is the Ever Shining Light in Darkness. Let His Light shine within you. He must be welcomed in by your heart, as our God can't rule within a hardened heart.

Our God is a God that Lives Inside of Us. He deposited a piece of His Holy Spirit inside of us. We are children of God. When the Holy Spirit of Jesus is on fire within us, then there is nothing He can't do through us.

Our God is our Rock and Solid Foundation. When your life is built upon Him, then everything falls into place.

Our God is our Prince of Peace Ruling in Our Hearts. He rules out fears, rules out shame, rules out guilt and hurt, rules out anxieties and brings clarity, calmness, confidence, security, reassurance, hope and faith that **He is God.**

This short verse, *"Be still and know that I am God,"* is far more than just eight simple words…

It's a promise letter from God.

It's a commitment oath from God.

It's a daily reminder from God for us to *Be Still,* and know that *He. Is. God.*

ACKNOWLEDGMENTS

Thank you to everyone below for continually inspiring me... whether you know it or not

Jesus

Brian Pasch

Mom and Dad

Fran Pasch

Christian Andrews

Paul Schnell

David and Loni Metter

Family and friends

Family and friends in Italy

Keira and Adam Smallcombe

Kim and Vance Roush

Entire Vive Church Family

Kevin Myers

DawnCheré and Rich Wilkerson

Rick Warren

Judah Smith

Carl Lentz

Charlotte Gambill

Christine Caine

Julie and Todd Mullins

Lisa Bevere

Lucille Houston

Wendy Perez

ABOUT THE AUTHOR

Carrie H. Pasch's writings are personal reflections from her daily quiet time of reading the Bible, journaling, and spending time with God. This is her first published work. This book was published with the purpose of helping people strengthen their relationship with God and to bring to life scripture lessons and verses from the Bible that impacted her walk with Christ.

Carrie and Brian Pasch reside in Florida and spend their summers on the New Jersey shore. Constantly traveling, the couple seeks to serve God wherever He has placed them. With frequent trips to Italy, Carrie has become fluent in the Italian language. She hopes one day to write a book in Italian and help be part of a revival in Italy.

CPSIA information can be obtained
at www.ICGtesting.com
Printed in the USA
LVHW081552281019
635578LV00015B/898/P